infant
stimuli

A complete program of
mental and physical stimulation
and devlopment
from birth to one year

P	rogram for
A	wareness of
R	ight and
E	arly
N	urturing of
T	he baby's
S	enses

Dr. J. Mansoor M.D.

www.infantstimuli.com

Editing: Len Coates
Book Design & Co-author: Neena Shaal
Printing and binding: Transcontinental Printing Inc. Canada.

Published by Infant Stimuli Canada Inc.
9A, 5205 Glen Erin Dr,
Mississauga, Ontario L5M 5N6

ISBN Number 0-9732946-0-4

For more information on products, visit

www.infantstimuli.com

ॐ

They made me smile when I cried
They picked me up when I stumbled
They put me on the right path when I went wrong
They showed me the light of knowledge and direction

To my Mother and Father for their intelligent
and dedicated parenting and selfless love

ॐॐ

Thanks to my loving family for their help and support.

❧

Special thanks to all the graphic designers and editors
for their hard work.

❧

Thanks to all the parents and babies who modeled to
make this book more beautiful and complete.

❧

Thanks to all the friends and relatives who
encouraged me to achieve this project.

❧

Table of contents

Introduction 7

1. Pregnancy and the Fetus 13

2. Fetus in the Womb 25

3. Nature and Nurture 37

4. The Vital Vision 45

5. Harmonious Hearing 57

6. The Tender Touch 65

7. Sensational Smell 73

8. The Joy of Taste 81

9. Speech and Language 87

10. Masyog (Massage & Yoga) 101

11. Balancing and Rocking 137

12. Magical Music 145

13. Sign Language 153

14. Intelligent Brain 167

15. The Amazing Right Brain 183

17. Milestones in the first year of life 197

The Stimulation Program 229

19. The First Quarter 233
    (1st, 2nd & 3rd month)

20. The Second Quarter 277
    (4th, 5th & 6th month)

21. The Third Quarter 307
    (7th, 8th & 9th month)

22. The Fourth Quarter 331
    (10th, 11th & 12th month)

Introduction

৪৩

A newborn baby is the most amazing bundle of joy. I have been dealing with babies for the last 27 years, yet whenever I examine a newborn, I stop and wonder about this beautiful creation of nature.

Babies grow very rapidly after birth, both physically as well as mentally.

The first three years are the most important in moulding the entire future life of an individual. The environment in which the babies are reared has a direct reflection on how they turn out in the future.

I have always had a great interest in developmental pediatrics. The benefits of proper nurturing of babies right from the time of birth prompted me to write about this subject. The objective is to create awareness among young parents about the benefits of good and early nurturing of the vital senses and the brain of their infant.

The information and techniques contained in this program are written in a simple language for the benefit of all parents and care givers.

The Infant Stimuli Program has been given the name:

PARENTS

P rogram for

A wareness of

R ight and

E arly

N urturing of

T he baby's

S enses

The Infant Stimuli Program covers the entire first year of life of the infant. It has been divided into four quarters, each quarter comprising of three months.

The detailed program is easy to practice because of the user-friendly tools and techniques.

The aim of this program is to rear intelligent babies, who will become better thinkers, good decision makers and emotionally happy adults.

A tremendous amount of research has been conducted over the last few years on the human brain and its capabilities. A lot of new and important information is now available regarding the functioning of the brain and mental faculties. Research has provided valuable insight into the vital senses of the brain and the way babies progress and develop from the time of conception until birth and into early childhood.

Valuable research has led us to some amazing facts regarding how babies hear, smell, see, and even have a memory, not only at birth, but even while still in the mother's womb. Thanks to the dedicated researchers in this field, we can now offer our children a better and a brighter future.

While the baby is in the mother's womb, the brain tissue is the center of phenomenal activity. As many as 250,000 cells form every minute. The brain of a newborn contains 100 billion brain cells. In the first year of life, the brain grows at a much faster rate than it will at any other time.

By six months of age, the infant's brain is half the weight of the adult brain. It grows to 70% by the end of one year and a staggering 90% by three years of age. The majority of brain growth occurs in the first three years of life, especially in the first year. This therefore makes the first three years of life, and more importantly the first year, the most crucial and precious time for the development of the brain.

The 100 billion nerve cells will form trillions of connections with each other in the first three years of life. It is through these connections that cells are able to communicate with each other and integrate the functioning of the various vital senses. Without these connections it would be impossible for the body to function.

Introduction

Connections between nerve cells cease to form after the first three years of life. The quality and the quantity of these connections will depend entirely on the amount and the intensity of the stimulation that the brain will receive.

Nature and Nurture go hand in hand, but nurturing the child in a proper manner goes a long way in determining the eventual intelligence and the capabilities of an individual.

It is important to remember that after about one and a half years of age, neural connections that are not being used will begin to die. Only those connections that are being nourished, nurtured and reinforced will flourish and thrive. Good quality stimulation and proper training of the brain is absolutely essential in the first few years of life.

It is a known fact that the average person uses only 4% of the brain during his/her life time. Intelligent stimulation in the first few years can lead to a substantial increase in the IQ level. Poor stimulation in the early years of life can lead to irreversible damage to intelligence and development.

While the brain is growing at a fast pace there are periods of learning called "The Critical Windows of Opportunities." These Critical Windows exist for all the important senses and are set periods during which learning occurs at a very rapid pace and with effortless ease.

The Critical Windows of Opportunities for vital senses such as vision, hearing, language and speech have certain important time frames, when they open one by one.

This happens in the first few months of life. Later, these windows of opportunities will close, one by one, and in a particular order. We must take full advantage of these critical windows while they are open because, once closed shut, they will not open again.

Memories of early childhood remain implanted in our brains forever. I was not surprised when I heard my 73-year-old mother getting irritated and complaining about forgetting events of the recent past. At the same time, she clearly remembered and related the events of her childhood, and even remembered the names of all her childhood friends and neighbors.

In 1981, the knowledge about the right brain and its capabilities came to light, when professor Roger Sperry of California Institute of Technology, received the Nobel Prize for his research on the functions of the right brain. Continued research has shown that the right brain has some amazing qualities, such as photographic memory or the ability to memorize large pieces of information at a very rapid speed.

Special emphasis is now being placed on the faculties of the right brain from very early in life. It has been found that the abilities of the right brain diminish as the child grows up.

It becomes very hard to make use of its wonderful capabilities after the age of six years.

Most infant educators believe that all babies are born Super Intelligent. It is up to parents and care givers to nurture and develop their abilities from the very early years.

Introduction

The first three years of life are the most critical years and have a direct reflection on the intelligence and development of a child. Experiences in early infancy can have an everlasting impression on the emotional makeup and behavior of an individual.

Hence good experiences and good stimulation add up to a healthy and intelligent personality.

Let us have faith in ourselves, our babies and their abilities.

Let us commit ourselves toward fulfilling our duties and our moral obligations toward our children and be proud parents.

Let us together, create and raise intelligent and happy generations.

෬෭

* To refrain from being biased toward the gender of babies 'She' and 'He' have been used in alternate chapters and quarters of the program.

* To emphasize the importance of stimulation, a few techniques have been repeated in all quarters .

Chapter 1

PREGNANCY AND THE FETUS

PREGNANCY AND THE FETUS

Conception is the beginning of a very close and intricate relationship between two human beings in which one is totally dependent on the other for its existence. In this case, it is the fetus that is totally dependent on the mother and the uterine conditions while inside the womb.

It is therefore vital for the mother to carry out this responsibility in a manner that provides the best possible conditions for the growth and development of the fetus.

Remember, the fetus inside the womb is there not by his or her own choice but by your choice. It is therefore the inherent right of the fetus to be provided with the best possible growing conditions within the womb.

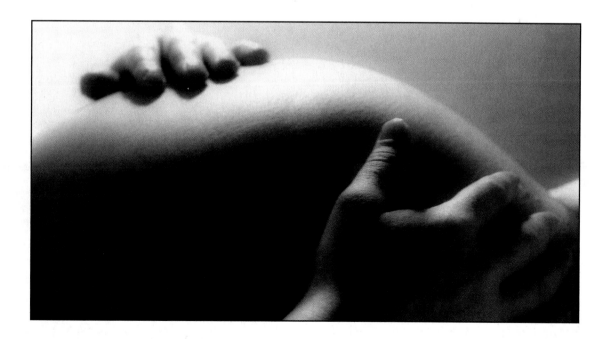

Pregnancy and the Fetus

Good and adequate care by the mother during the important period of pregnancy will nurture the physical and mental growth of the baby to the optimum, which in turn will enable him to grow into a healthy, happy, stable and intelligent human being.

Congenital malformations, premature delivery and many other conditions can have a profound effect on the baby's future life. Factors that can lead to these conditions should therefore be very well recognized and avoided.

Experiences of the fetus while in the mother's womb can have an everlasting impression on his personality.

It is therefore important to provide a healthy and a happy environment for the baby while he is developing in the uterus.

Some of the important factors that have an effect on the growing fetus are as follows:

1. MATERNAL NUTRITION

2. EFFECTS OF DRUGS AND MEDICATION

3. ALCOHOL AND SUBSTANCE ABUSE

4. MATERNAL INFECTIONS

MATERNAL NUTRITION

The developing fetus is entirely dependent on the mother for nutrition. Essential vitamins, minerals and all the other good nutrients are vital for the fetus to grow properly. All this nutrition has to come from the mother through the umbilical cord to the baby. The quality of food that the mother consumes during pregnancy is of great importance. The diet should be good, healthy and well balanced.

Close attention to maternal nutrition should begin as soon as the pregnancy is planned. The brain and nervous tissue of the fetus will grow at a startling rate from the fourth month onward. As we know, the brain is an extremely important and vital organ of the body and its rapid growth makes it critically important to provide adequate nutrition.

Deficiency or low intake of calcium, iron, iodine and vitamins, especially the B12 vitamin, over prolonged periods during pregnancy can lead to low birth-weight babies. Inadequate nutrition of the mother can lead to learning disabilities, delay in language development, behavioral problems and a lower IQ in infants.

It can also result in delayed development of motor skills. Undernourished fetuses are at a greater risk of illnesses in later life because of poor resistance.

One of the most severe birth defects is related to a deficiency of folic acid, which is a B-complex vitamin. A deficiency of folic acid leads to failure of the neural tube to close properly.

The neural tube is the tissue from which the brain and the spinal cord develop. Improper closing of the tube can give rise to severe malformations of the brain or the spinal cord.

The neural tube closes as early as 22 to 28 days after conception, a time when most women don't even know that they are pregnant.

Folic acid is found in green leafy vegetables, broccoli, beans, citrus fruits and liver. The importance of folic acid intake during pregnancy is so universally accepted that health authorities now recommend that all women likely to get pregnant should consume 0.4milligrams of folic acid every day.

EFFECTS OF DRUGS AND MEDICATION

As a rule, medication should be avoided during pregnancy. The medicines taken by the mother can enter the fetal circulation through the placenta and can affect the developing fetus.

Even drugs sold over the counter should not be taken without proper medical advice.

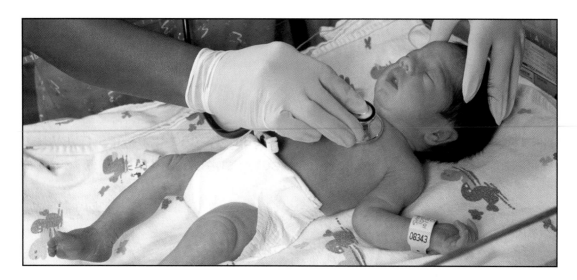

A simple medicine such as aspirin taken a few days prior to delivery can cause bleeding in a child's brain because of its ability to inhibit blood clotting.

It is best to seek medical advice before taking any medication, especially in the first trimester of pregnancy when the baby's organs and systems are being formed.

One of the most disastrous effects of medication occurred in the late fifties when women were prescribed Thalidomide to stop vomiting in early pregnancy. Use of Thalidomide resulted in the birth of many babies with severe congenital malformations. These included gross physical abnormalities such as missing limbs, blindness and hearing loss.

Similarly, exposure to radiation and chemical agents can also affect the pregnant mother as well as the growing fetus.

ALCOHOL AND SUBSTANCE ABUSE

Since there are no specific parameters available for the safe level of alcohol during pregnancy, it is advisable to abstain from alcohol as soon as the pregnancy is planned.

Alcohol crosses the placenta very quickly and reaches a level in the bloodstream of the fetus directly comparable to the level of alcohol in the mother's bloodstream.

Therefore, the baby of a mother consuming alcohol is as intoxicated as the mother herself.

Pregnancy and the Fetus

We all know the harmful effects of alcohol, even in adults. It slows down the mental faculties, impairs concentration and leads to other behavioral disorders. So you can well imagine the damaging effects of alcohol on the fragile and developing brain tissue of a baby.

Of all the body organs, brain tissue is the most sensitive and vulnerable to the ill effects of alcohol.

Heavy drinking during pregnancy has been linked to fetal abnormalities, and many of these babies suffer from FAS (Fetal Alcohol Syndrome).

They are born with a smaller head and underdeveloped brain and have a lower IQ level. Associated with FAS are also abnormalities of the eyes, malformation of the face, stunted physical growth and congenital heart disease.

Even social drinking, such as consumption of a glass or two of wine a day by the mother during pregnancy, will result in the child having a lower intelligence quotient, poor attention span and deficits in cognitive skills and motor functions.

The most damaging effects on the fetus due to alcohol consumption are caused in the first few weeks of pregnancy.

COCAINE:

Babies born to mothers with cocaine addiction tend to be smaller with low birth weight. They are also at an increased risk of having a congenital abnormality of the skull called microcephaly.

In this condition, the skull is very small, and there is no room for the brain to grow. This can result in severe mental retardation. Use of cocaine by pregnant mothers also increases the risk of haemorrhage in the infant's brain, which can again result in irreversible brain damage.

HEROIN:

Babies born to mothers who are dependent on heroin will usually exhibit withdrawal symptoms as if they have been addicted to the drug themselves.

There is also a high rate of neonatal deaths of babies in this group, and they suffer from various behavioral and social disorders.

MARIJUANA:

Babies born to mothers who use marijuana during pregnancy show behavioral and other emotional problems as they grow up.

They have problems with speech and language and can develop memory disorders. As marijuana is smoked, babies born to addicted mothers suffer from the effects of the drug as well as complications arising from smoking.

TOBACCO:

Although tobacco smoking has not been proven to produce structural defects in the fetus, it has however been found to have harmful effects in other ways. Nicotine from the smoke causes constriction of blood vessels, reducing blood flow and nutrition to the placenta and affecting the fetus.

Since the developing fetus is deprived of essential nutrition, the babies of smoking mothers tend to be born with low birth weight. Smoking reduces the level of oxygen and increases carbon monoxide in the blood of the mother as well as that of the fetus.

CAFFEINE:

Caffeine is found in coffee, tea and cola. Although there is no evidence that caffeine causes congenital malformations, some studies have shown that consumption of caffeine in large doses increases the rate of spontaneous abortions.

It also increases the chances of babies being born with low birth weight. It is therefore advisable to limit caffeine intake during pregnancy.

MATERNAL INFECTIONS

Fortunately, most pregnant women today are aware of the hazards of self-medication, alcohol, radiation and drug abuse. Because of this knowledge, the incidence of congenital malformations has been on the decline.

However, the danger from various maternal infections during pregnancy is still a matter of concern. Many of these infections can pass off as trivial illnesses without causing significant clinical symptoms.

RUBELLA:

Rubella virus causes German measles. As an illness it may show very mild symptoms in the mother and in some cases may even go unnoticed.

However, the effects of rubella on the developing fetus can be devastating.

The rubella virus can cause severe mental retardation, hearing loss, and cataracts in the eyes of the infant. It can give rise to severe malformations in as many as 50 percent of cases if the mother contracts the infection in the first month of pregnancy.

The incidence of these defects from the infection, however, declines as the pregnancy progresses.

Fortunately, most child-bearing females are already immunized against Rubella and they usually have blood screening done to determine their immunity level as soon as they get pregnant.

CYTOMEGALOVIRUS:

This virus can be transmitted through saliva, blood, urine, semen and other bodily fluids. Personal hygiene is therefore very important for pregnant women. CMV may produce little or no symptoms at all in the pregnant woman but has severe consequences such as mental retardation and deafness in the fetus, especially if infected in the first two trimesters of pregnancy.

TOXOPLASMOSIS:

This parasite can infect a pregnant woman through feces of cats or from eating raw meat or eggs. The illness might be very mild in the mother but can give rise to mental retardation, epilepsy, blindness or hearing disorders in the newborn.

SYPHILIS:

Screening for syphilis during early pregnancy helps to avoid severe complications in the brain, eyes, bones, skin and liver of the newborns.

GENITAL HERPES:

Usually this infection is transmitted to the baby during the birth process. Babies that get infected with this virus can become very ill and have a risk of severe brain damage if the infection is not treated promptly.
In some rare cases, genital herpes can be transmitted to the fetus while still inside the mother's womb and can give rise to brain, eye and skin disorders. Once again, this illness can be diagnosed and treated fairly easily earlier on in pregnancy.

The first three years of life are the most crucial years for the development of the brain, and out of these, the first year is essentially the most important.

❀❀❀❀❀❀❀❀❀❀

Chapter 2

FETUS IN THE WOMB

Fetus in the Womb

All human beings want love, care and attention. If we get love and affection, we feel happy and confident and are able to function better.

From the time of conception until birth, the baby spends nine lonely months in the mother's womb living in solitary confinement. The baby needs a mother's company, love, care and attention all the time.

The mental attitude of the woman and her psychological state during pregnancy have a lot to do with the development of the fetus inside.

Stress-free living conditions and a stable emotional state of the parents goes a long way in enhancing the prospects for having a healthy and a happy baby.

Women who have shown love and care for the baby throughout pregnancy will have babies who are healthier, happier and relaxed.

Whereas, if one had wanted a termination of pregnancy or did not really want to have the baby, it will usually result in children with low birth weight and behavioral problems.

Fetus in the Womb

When a mother is under stress during pregnancy, she secretes undesirable hormones that pass through the placenta and have a negative effect on the growing baby.

It is no surprise to anyone that fetuses respond to the mother's heartbeat and her voice in the latter part of pregnancy. By his reactions, fetus shows that he is sensitive to light from the 16th week of pregnancy. Hearing is developed from the 24th week onward.

Researchers have found that the first streaks of memory start developing in the brain at some point during the third trimester of pregnancy. The mother's womb is the first institution of learning.

Incredible studies have been conducted on adults under hypnosis, and the subjects have been able to recall incidents while they were in the mother's womb. Some can even narrate the process of their birth in great detail.

The brain cells are forming at a startling rate in the first few weeks of pregnancy. We know that by the fifth month of pregnancy the number of cells that the baby's brain will eventually have has already been determined. After that time, the brain cells continue to grow in size but not in numbers.

Not only is the brain growing in size, but the ability to process feelings and emotions also starts by the second trimester of pregnancy.

Apart from emotions, the ability to manifest feelings of anxiety and feelings of anger are also developing in the brain of the fetus. With all this activity going on, one can understand the importance of the stimuli that are being offered to the fetus by the mother and the environment.

Bonding between the mother and the newborn is now a well-known fact. With our knowledge of the capabilities of the fetus, importance is being placed on the science and art of prebonding, which is bonding between the mother and the fetus prior to birth.

It has been well established that the mother can communicate with the child within the womb. This proves the bonding process of love and affection between the two can start long before the baby is born.

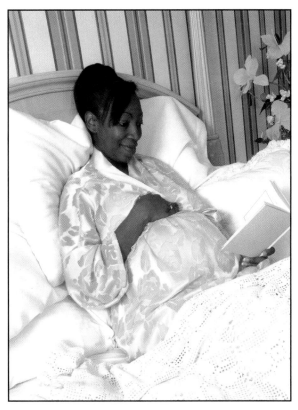

It is therefore important for the mother to talk in a gentle, caring and loving manner with the fetus.

You will be amazed at the influence this communication and bonding can have on the emotional and intellectual development of the baby.

It is a desire of every human being to be wanted and loved. Why should the fetus be any different?

In fact, he needs all the reassurance, warmth, love and affection in his tiny little room where he is confined alone for the first nine months of his life. It is comforting and reassuring for him to know that there are people around who want him and love him.

Since one has already laid the foundation of pre-birth bonding with the baby while he is still in the womb, it makes bonding at birth much easier and more effective.

Intense, abundant and good quality communication with the developing fetus is the indicator of an intelligent, healthy and happy baby in the future.

If the mother has been talking to the baby during her pregnancy in a loving manner, the child is born with a happier and more stable personality.

The fetus may not understand the meanings of what is being said but certainly absorbs all the emotion that accompanies the speech. In this way, the mother starts to shape the emotional characteristics of the baby even before he arrives in this world.

Useful Techniques:

- One of the earliest and best ways that a fetus learns is by listening to the mother's voice. It is a great idea to make an audio tape and play it to the fetus throughout the last months of the pregnancy. It is ideal to have both parents' voices recorded for about five minutes duration each.

- Communication with the baby inside the womb is very important. Each parent should take turns talking to the baby, narrating a story, recounting the experiences of the day, or even reading a nursery rhyme. They should use gentle tones, and tell the baby how much they love him.

The positive effects of prebirth bonding have been clearly demonstrated by researchers through a study conducted using the recording of the mother's heart beat.

These recordings have proved to settle and calm down irritable and anxious newborns. It has been known that these babies thrive well, gain weight and are happier and healthier physically and emotionally after birth.

I personally experienced this, while sitting with my irritated grandchild on a swing one evening. He quickly settled down in my arms as we started to go back and forth. To my surprise, it was not the movement but the click, click noise that the swing was making. The click mimicked the sound of the regular heartbeat of his mother. This calmed him down to the extent that he fell asleep.

Another fascinating fact is that the foundation of language is laid down in the brain while the fetus is still in the mother's womb. Time and again, it is been proved that newborns prefer to hear the language that they have heard regularly while inside the womb, as compared to another language.

There have been amazing examples of how a child could speak words from a language other than the mother tongue. Invariably, this had been picked up by the fetus's brain from the languages spoken around the mother's work or social environment, while she was carrying the baby in the womb.

Music is another sound that babies like to hear and enjoy even long before they are born. Infants born prematurely gain weight faster, fight infections much better and thrive well when exposed to music while being treated in intensive care units.

Exposure to music reduces emotional stress in irritated babies. It speeds up motor development and enhances other important skills such as reading and writing.

Children who listen to classical music on a regular basis have advanced mathematical capabilities. These children also tend to have a higher IQ at a later stage in life, as compared to other children of the same age group, who were not exposed to music.

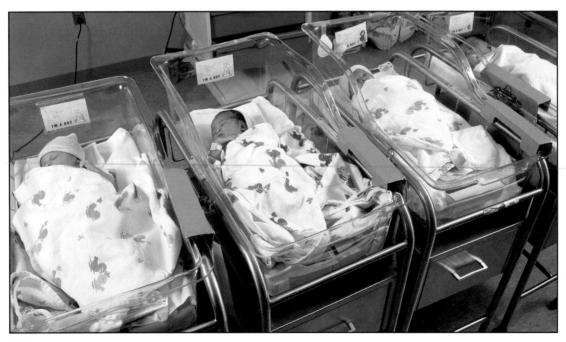

Effects of Maternal Stress on the Fetus

There are two kinds of mothers. One is, who plans a pregnancy and definitely wants to have the baby. The other mother is the one, who never really wanted to have a baby and rejected the baby during pregnancy.

The former mothers will be communicating with their fetuses better and will be giving a lot of emotional support to them in a positive and loving atmosphere. These babies will be both emotionally and physically healthier and happier.

The latter mothers will not have developed any bonding with the baby before or even after birth. Such babies invariably will not only be lagging behind in physical development, but in many cases will grow up with emotional and behavioral disorders.

Let us now look at another very important aspect of pregnancy, the mental harmony and happiness of the mother during pregnancy. Any severe and persistent emotional distress to the mother during her pregnancy has significant effects, such as continued and prolonged periods of anxiety and emotional stress.

This may be due to any number of reasons, such as emotional setbacks, financial reversals and other social constraints during this period.

When these prolonged stresses take place within the mother, there is an increase in maternal neurohormonal production.

Neurohormones are chemical substances produced by the body in response to certain emotional and anxiety states that we encounter. These substances produce an altered state of the human body and behavior.

These neurohormones, if produced in excess amounts in the mother, will cross over from the mother's bloodstream to the fetus and have a negative impact on the developing brain of the baby.

Such a phenomenon can actually change the developing child's physiological as well as the psychological composition.

Similarly, if the mother is in a happy and a relaxed state of mind and body, the hormone composition of her system will be good thereby, having a positive effect on the mind and the brain of the developing baby.

It is relevant to say here "like mother, like fetus." These four words sum up and signify the importance of the direct relationship between the emotional and psychological makeup of the mother and the baby she is carrying inside the womb.

Father and the Fetus

Most views and discussion start with the bonding role of the mother with the baby. Let us pause here for a moment and take a look at the father's role during pregnancy.

Just how important is his role with relation to the emotional and physical well-being of the fetus and the newborn?

The father's temperament, his behavior, the tone of his voice and the emotional concern for the mother and the baby certainly have a bearing in determining the emotional well being of the fetus.

This also has a direct effect on the formation of his emotional traits after birth.

It is a known fact that angry and screaming fathers provoke the fetus to the extent that he becomes agitated and kicks vigorously in the womb, clearly showing his displeasure.

The state of happiness of the mother, her mental well being and relationship with the father of her unborn child have a direct and important influence on the emotional development of the fetus.

Happy couples always produce happy and emotionally sound babies, whereas unhappy parents produce emotionally and psychologically handicapped babies.

Useful Techniques:

- Play the recording of a loving conversation of the father to the fetus a few times a day in the last three months of pregnancy.
- The father should place his hand on the mother's tummy while narrating a story to the baby or singing a song or lullaby.
- Father should always be gentle and loving with the mother because those vibrations and messages are passed on directly to the unborn baby.

Can you imagine the delightful emotional configuration of a child who as a fetus, has received all the love and care from both mother and father while developing inside the mother's womb?

It is astonishing and amazing to see the reaction and the expression on the newborn's face when, moments after birth, the father speaks aloud in person and repeats the contents of the recordings which were played to him while in the womb.

The newborn will actually raise his head and turn toward the sound of his father's voice, even if it is relayed from different directions in the delivery room.

Conclusively, therefore, it is not only the mother's, but the father's bonding as well that shapes the fetus's mind and personality.

The more loving and caring the atmosphere around the baby in the womb, the better person he will be in the outside world.

Chapter 3

Nature
and
Nurture

Nature and Nurture

What is intelligence?

This has forever been a matter of debate. Various definitions are being put forward all the time. Scholars and educators have had their own interpretations and views on the subject. The unanimous view, however, is that intelligence is not a physical commodity that can be measured in pounds or kilos.

It is an abstract entity yet something so obvious that anyone can make out the difference between a knowledgeable person and a person with limited or no knowledge.

My personal definition is that intelligence is the ability to absorb, verify, interpret, deduce and apply knowledge or information. Knowledge therefore forms the basis of intelligence.

The more knowledge one has, the more intelligent he or she is to be considered. Indeed, it is so very often that we refer to a well-read and well-informed person as an intelligent individual.

Genes and inheritance do play an important role in the intelligence of an individual. The level of intelligence that a person is going to acquire from the parents is already determined at the time of conception.

How important is the inheritance of intelligence?

Let us analyze in more detail the role inheritance plays in the development of intelligence in an individual. At this point, I recall a personal experience of mine. I once lived near a beautiful park with a lake and a bird sanctuary.

Nature and Nurture

This was a very popular retreat for many people, especially during the weekends. I always noticed a lot of gardeners looking after the flower beds, watering the plants, neatly mowing the lush green grass and pruning the beautiful tall trees.

The park was well known for its beauty and lovely surroundings. I used to visit this place often in the summers and always enjoyed a relaxing day out, admiring the beauty of nature.

However, when the time came to drive back home I would always feel sad.

This was because my return journey was through an overgrown bushy pathway. I always wondered, what makes these two pieces of land lying so close to each other so different.

The answer was plain and simple. The park was well looked after, well cared for and well nourished, whereas the pathway was left only to nature to take care of.

Nature certainly provided the nourishment to all the bushes and shrubs on the pathway, but there was no one nurturing those unruly and overgrown trees and shrubs. On the other hand, the park was well looked after and properly nurtured.

You might have visited some awesome flower shows and exhibitions. It is always the most nurtured and well-cultivated rose that will win the prize. Nature has given us abundance of intelligence right at birth and we must nurture it properly and carefully.

The human brain is a product of nature, and nurturing the brain can make all the difference in the eventual functioning of this vital organ.

On many occasions, I have come across babies who have been adopted at birth and nurtured in an intelligent environment. It is incredible and unbelievable to see these children when they are a few years old. The comparison between the adopted child's personality and intelligence level is quite different than her biological sibling who did not have the same opportunities. Remember both these siblings did inherit similar intelligence through the genetic transmission from the biological parents. One was obviously nurtured better than the other.

The surroundings have a great impact on the growing brain and the other vital senses of the human being.

A classic example and a very important one in the context of nurturing is the example of a girl named Genie.

She was made a captive and kept in solitary confinement since the age of 20 months by her psychotic father in their suburban home in Los Angeles.

She did not have anybody to communicate with and there was no contact with the outside world. Genie led a life all alone for 12 years, until her mother finally managed to escape with her.

Unfortunately, the damage had already been done by then. She could barely walk, and her eyes could not focus beyond a distance of 12 feet. She could not chew or swallow food properly. She could not understand or speak any language.

Although she received intensive medical attention and rehabilitation for many years after her freedom, her physical and mental milestones lagged far behind normal.

Her language, despite great efforts, could not progress much beyond that of a two-year-old child.

This story is the living example of the effect that early nurturing has on the entire life of a person.

Deprivation of proper stimulation will always lead to irreversible damage to intelligence.

Dr. Warren Dennis conducted a study in 1960 on infants that were being brought up in an orphanage.

Apart from being fed, these children received minimal contact and received very little stimulation from their environment.

At the age of two years, the results were shocking and devastating. Sixty percent of these children at age two could not sit unsupported and lacked in all spheres of their physical and mental development.

Their growth was stunted and they were way behind normal in their motor development, intelligence and other mental faculties. Most of this damage was irreversible.

Therefore, proper nurturing at the right time is of great importance in all infants and growing children.

People who have trained their minds to work faster and better have to spend far less time achieving results than others. The human brain is like an uncut and unpolished diamond. To realize its true potential, it has to be nurtured and stimulated in a proper way and at the right time.

Most of us firmly believe that we are born with a certain amount of intelligence by virtue of our genes and we will have to do with that for the rest of our lives.

If we had left everything to inheritance and genes, then all educators, scientists and discoverers would be born only in super intelligent households. In my personal experience, many highly successful and brilliant colleagues of mine came from families with average intelligence. These people however were the ones who nurtured their brains very well and enhanced their intelligence to be outstanding in their professions and their lives.

Many researches have indicated that an average person throughout his or her lifetime uses only 4 percent of the brain. The more one can learn to use the brain effectively, the greater the level of intelligence will be. Trying to optimize the ability of the brain to function comes with practice and by the stimulation that the brain gets earlier on in life.

Nature and Nurture

The development of an infant's brain is like the foundation of a building, the stronger the foundation the sturdier the building will be.

Do not be afraid to enlighten the brain of an infant as much as you can. It is like a sponge and will absorb anything with ease. We are afraid to teach our little ones because we think we are pushing them too hard. If one is using only 4 percent of the entire brain, where does the burden come from? Even the simplest of machines, if run at 4 percent of its capacity, can never get tired or worn out. On the other hand if the brain is trained early enough, it will function better and smarter and eventually formal education at school becomes much easier.

Nurturing the brain should start as soon as the baby is born. Proper stimulation should be provided to all the vital senses such as vision, hearing, speech and language.
It is important to start early. The first three years of life are critical for the developing brain.

It is during these three years that the brain grows at a rapid pace and the brain cells are forming interconnections with one another at a startling rate. This is also the time when the right brain is very active and dominant.

Stimulation of the right brain will develop qualities such as photographic memory and the ability to memorize large quantities of information with ease.

Proper early stimulation will give children a head start and contribute greatly toward developing them into intelligent adults.

XXXXXXX

Chapter 4

Vital Vision

The Vital Vision

When the human eye looks at an object, light rays pass through the lens and fall on the retina which is located at the back of the eyeball. The retina has two types of specialized nerve cells which are called rods and cones. Rods are more sensitive to light. These cells are located more peripherally on the retina. Since they are sensitive to light and are placed peripherally on the retina, rods play an important role in night vision and peripheral vision.

The other types of cells on the retina, called the cones, are placed along the center part of the retina. These cells are responsible for color vision and primarily recognize blue, green and red. The visual system can blend these colors in varying proportion and can recognize a wide spectrum of many others colors from this basic color bank.

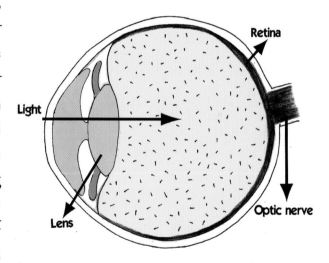

The first optic tissue in the fetus appears as two tiny little blobs placed on the sides and at the front end of the neural tube. This happens as early as 22 days after conception. During the first five weeks, these blobs have changed into cup-shaped structures and have also differentiated into the lens and the retina of the eye.

These blobs then migrate toward the midline by about eight weeks of fetal life. The retina or the image-capturing screen located at the back of the eye is developed between the 6th and the 20th week of gestation.

The nerve that transmits light from the eye to the brain is called the optic nerve. It is formed by the eighth week of gestation.

By 27 weeks of gestation, the fetal brain starts responding to stimulation by light.

Once an image has been perceived by the retina, the message is carried by the optic nerve and reaches the primary visual cortex in the brain. The primary visual cortex is the place where all information about an image is processed. It is located at the rear of the brain.

The visual cortex undergoes massive growth between 14 and 28 weeks of gestation. Because of the complexity of the visual system and the amount of information to be processed, such as depth, dimensions, movements and color, it is not surprising that the brain devotes more area to the visual sense than to all the other vital senses combined.

In a new-born baby, the eye is about one-third of its adult size. The basic elements of the visual system are present but not fully matured. The lens and the central part of the retina where the receptors are located is still immature, and the movements of the eyes are also not well coordinated.

ର Newborns can clearly see within a distance of 13 inches from their faces. The peripheral vision is narrow at birth, but starts to develop rapidly within a few weeks.

The infant's vision starts to improve quickly as the eye muscles, the lens, retina and the eye/brain connection start to mature. At about two months of age both the eyes are starting to function together.

Visual acuity in an adult is 20/20. The visual acuity of 20/20 in an adult means that he can see and clearly identify an object 20 feet away from him. If an individual has a visual acuity of 20/50, which is not normal, it means that he can see an object clearly from a distance of 20 feet compared to a person with normal visual acuity who will be able to see the same object clearly from a distance of 50 feet.

At birth, the infant's acuity is about 20/400, but it starts to improve very quickly during the first year of life as a result of changes in the brain and the neural connections. By one year of age, most infants reach a level of 20/20 which means it is now as good as that of an adult.

For the first few weeks of life, infants best see black and white. By two months of age, however, the ability to distinguish between different colors is quite good, but color vision is still in a rudimentary stage.

As weeks go by, they can see farther and farther, and by three months, can easily see objects within a distance of 10 feet.

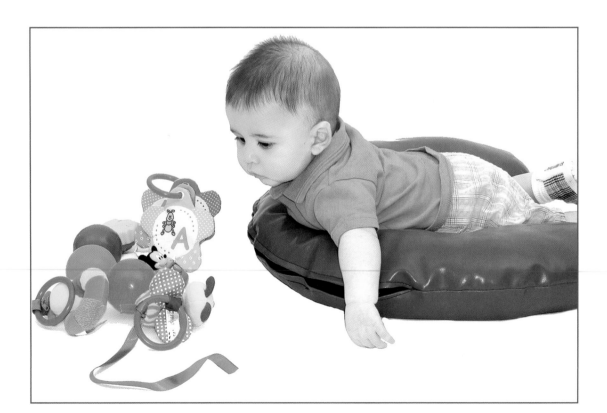

Despite the ability to focus only a short distance at birth, newborns actively scan their surroundings. Newborns like to look at different geometric shapes and enjoy looking at complex patterns, such as checkerboards, concentric circles and stripes, rather than plain patterns. They seem to concentrate more on black and white and three dimensional objects and like to look and concentrate on areas of high contrast and at the edges between the shape and the background.

Newborns also have an affinity for human faces or even portraits of human faces drawn on a white background. A newborn has the ability to identify and recognize the mother's face as early as two days after birth.

.s a major spurt of activity in the visual system between four to eight months of the infant's life. This is what is called the "critical window of opportunity."

Visual stimulation should be carried out to the maximum during this phase of life, to create and strengthen as many connections as possible between the eye and the brain, both in terms of quality and quantity.

For the first few weeks newborns can best see black and white.

By 3 months of age infants can clearly see up to a distance of 10 feet.

Due to this early spurt of activity, the child's early visual experiences will leave a strong and a long-lasting impression as far as visual perception is concerned. Heredity does play a role in the quality of vision, but it is critical to remember that early visual stimulation and visual experiences play a major role in the child's eventual visual capabilities.

By four months of age, the special areas responsible for processing the color vision in the cortex are fully mature.

Normal development of vision requires that both the eyes function together. This is called binocular vision.

On average, binocular vision develops around three and a half months of age. Anything that prevents a child from using both the eyes together increases the risk of permanent visual defects, which may not be corrected later on. It is therefore important that babies who are showing signs of cross eyes be treated promptly.

Besides a problem occurring in the binocular vision, the other problem that could occur is the lack of clarity in vision. This may happen because of some opacity in the lens of the eye, which is known as a congenital cataract. If the opacity is not removed or corrected in time, it can lead to permanent visual disability.

This happens because the eye/brain connection was not stimulated at the right time, and the critical window of opportunity went to waste.

It is recommended that congenital cataracts be removed as soon as they are detected. If left untreated, and not removed by the age of six months, chances of achieving a reasonable amount of visual acuity in the future are slim. It is now a common procedure to remove cataracts as early as two months of age.

The attention span of a newborn can be increased from a few seconds to more than a minute by offering him visual stimulation in sharp contrasting black and white patterns. This ability of the newborn to gaze attentively at these patterns is called fixation.

The process of following a moving object within the visual field is called tracking. If the newborn is offered an object of interesting shape and contrast, he will track the object with more interest and for a longer duration.

The ability to track in the first few weeks of life is not very well developed but increases rapidly by the third month.

Using highly contrasting colors and interesting complex shapes

The critical window for the sense of vision is wide open from 4-8 months of age

as stimulation tools can greatly enhance the tracking ability of a newborn.

When an infant is presented with several different objects within his visual field, his eyes will show small jumping movements from one object to the other until they finally settle on the object of his choice. This is called **scanning**.
Scanning, tracking and fixation are all important components in the development and enhancement of visual abilities.

The human eye and the visual pathway are indeed one of the most fascinating areas of research in the medical field.

Now that we know about the timing of visual pathway development and the critical periods of eye/brain connection, every opportunity should be taken to provide the infant with rich experiences in visual stimulation. It not only enhances the visual pathway but at the same time stimulates and nurtures the infant's other vital senses.

> By the age of four months, the visual capability of an infant is comparable to that of an adult.

Chapter 5

Harmonious Hearing

Harmonious Hearing

Of all the senses, the sense of hearing is definitely the most important to the newborn. It is through hearing that the brain processes sounds and helps us to learn speech and language. Language is the primary tool of communication between human beings. Without this, life would be impossible.

It is through communication that we convey our thoughts to others and also receive information from the people around us. It is vital for the development of our intellect.

Hearing also plays a very important role in establishing coordination between vital senses such as vision, touch and smell.

A newborn's hearing is far more developed than the ability to see. The sense of hearing starts to develop while the fetus is in the womb. A fetus has the ability to recognize, register and respond to various sounds while in the womb.

Babies who have received a lot of verbal communication from the parents while in the womb will actually turn toward the parent's voices even minutes after birth.

Newborn babies show interest in hearing the language they were exposed to while still in the womb, compared to another language.

The human voice is the sound newborns like to hear most. Babies can recognize their mother's voice and can differentiate it from the voice of another person as early as three days after birth.

The ear is the primary organ for hearing. It is divided into three parts, the outer ear, the middle ear and the inner ear. Sound reaches the ear in the form of air waves. Nature has made the transmission of sound waves easier for us by ensuring that the outer ear and middle ear are full of air. This facilitates the transmission of sound waves. These waves enter the ear canal and strike the ear drum. When the ear drum is struck by sound waves, it starts to vibrate.

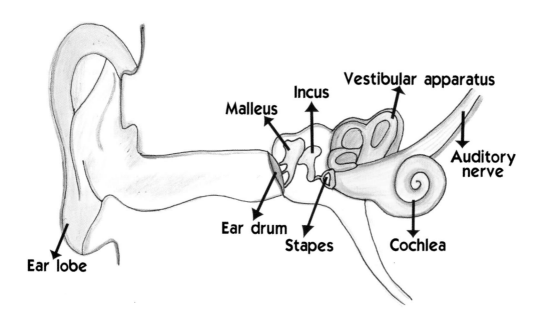

Beyond the ear drum is the middle ear. It contains three little bony structures, called the malleus, incus and the stapes. The vibration of the ear drum starts a series of waves in the middle ear. These waves hit the malleus, incus and the stapes, and they in turn start to vibrate. This sequence of vibration is then transmitted to another membrane in the middle ear which is called the oval window. This is the inner boundary of the middle ear.

Beyond the oval window is the inner ear. It is here that the organ of hearing called the auditory organ or cochlea is lodged. It is in the cochlea that the vibration of sound waves is converted into electrical signals. These signals are then carried from the cochlea through the auditory nerve to the hearing area in the brain. This is called the primary auditory region and is located around the temple area of the skull.

The earliest cells of the auditory system appear as early as three weeks after gestation. By six weeks, the auditory nerve is clearly formed.

The cochlea in the inner ear resembles a coiled structure, much like a snail, and is completely developed by the 11th week of gestation.

Since the fetus begins to hear as early as the 24th week of gestation, the sounds and language that she hears has a large impact on her development. She enjoys listening to her mother's voice and reacts to it.

The other sound that fascinates the fetus is the mother's heartbeat which is the first sound she heard and had been her constant companion inside the womb.

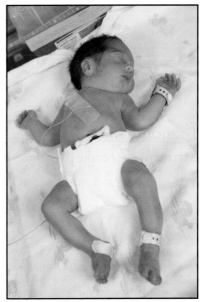

The maternal heartbeat is very comforting and soothing for babies, especially when they are agitated and restless.

So profound is the effect of the sound of maternal heartbeat, that a lot of intensive care units use it as a tool for treatment of critically ill babies.

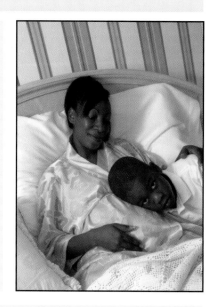

The sound of the maternal heart beat improves mental and physical development, and helps sick babies to fight infections better and gain weight faster.

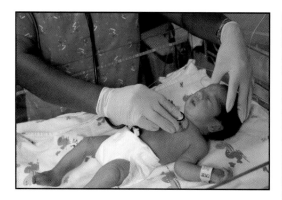

Now that we know the development of hearing begins so early in fetal life, it is the best means of stimulation for the rapidly growing brain of the baby.

Taking advantage of this knowledge, it is highly recommended that parents make the fetus listen to their voices and the voices of siblings as often as possible, especially in the last trimester of pregnancy.

This exercise creates and increases bonding between parents, siblings and the newborn child. It also plays a vital role in the emotional development of the baby.

Since we know and appreciate the importance of the vital sense of hearing, it is also critical to safeguard against certain mishaps that may lead to impairment of this particular sense during fetal development.

Babies can hear very well in the last trimester of the pregnancy. It is important to monitor the kind of sounds to which the unborn baby is exposed.

Studies reveal that mothers who work in noisy environments such as factories, expose their fetuses to a greater risk of hearing loss.

Normal human speech is at a frequency of 60 to 65 decibels. Newborns can hear sounds at 30 to 35 decibels. There is really no need for us to talk to babies in loud voices because we believe their sense of hearing is not well developed.
The soft, gentle, whispering tone of the mother's voice is more soothing and comforting to the baby than a loud voice.

With modern technology, hearing defects can be detected as early as six weeks after birth.

If the parents or caregiver suspect a hearing disturbance or a deficit, a hearing test can be carried out even on very small babies. This is done by placing earphones over the ears and electrodes over the scalp of the baby to record electrical activity of the auditory pathway.

One of the common conditions that can result in a hearing loss after birth in small babies is recurrent middle-ear infections. Fortunately, middle-ear infections in children can be diagnosed and treated fairly easily and early.

Proper stimulation of the vital sense of hearing is very important and should be carried out right from the third trimester of pregnancy.

Exposure to different sounds, abundance of language and soft music will enhance the listening capabilities of the infant. It speeds up the process of emotional development, emergence of the thought processes and intelligence.

The period between 4 to 10 months
of age is the critical window of opportunity for the sense of hearing.

Chapter 6

The Tender Touch

The Tender Touch

A newborn has the ability to detect sensation on the skin when touched. This is very simply exhibited by the movements of a child when he is tickled or touched.

Although the sense of touch is one of the baby's most advanced faculties at the time of birth, it still takes a long time before the baby can differentiate between various kinds of sensations.

The ability to feel at birth is far better than the ability to see or hear. The first sense to emerge in a developing embryo is that of touch, starting with the lips and the nose. These areas are sensitive to touch as early as the fifth or sixth week of gestation.

The sense of touch starts from the face and spreads down toward the toes. Around the ninth week of gestation, the eyelids, chin and arms can feel touch.

Legs start to feel touch by the 10th week, and by the 12th week of gestation, almost the entire body surface is sensitive to touch. The exceptions are the top and the back of the head, which do not show any sensation to touch throughout the period of gestation.

The sense of touch keeps developing after birth, and by the time the baby is one-year old, touch sensitivity and perception is four times better than that at birth.
Contrary to old belief, newborns certainly do react to pain. The sense of pain emerges sometime before the third trimester of pregnancy.

The skin has the ability at birth to sense pain if pinched or pricked. Since we know that newborns can feel pain, even minor surgical procedures must be carried out under proper local anesthesia or pain-free conditions. Baby's mouth is one of the first areas to become sensitive, so it's no wonder that all babies as soon they are able to grasp objects tend to put them into their mouth. Newborns can feel soft and firm, rough and smooth, hot and cold.

The five parts of the body that are highly sensitive to touch are the face, the area of the skin over the backbone, the genital area, palms and soles of the feet.

Regularly massaging or stroking these sensitive areas will greatly stimulate the neural pathway.

Touch is a unique sensation. It produces warmth and love, so much so that gentle stroking, hugging and talking to newborns makes a world of difference for the infant in the future.

Even as little as an intimate first hour of close skin contact between the newborn and the mother can leave an everlasting impression on the child.

As mentioned earlier in this book, the importance of touch was greatly highlighted by Dr. Warren Dennis, an American pediatrician who carried out a study of children being brought up in an orphanage. By the time the study was finished, some startling facts had been discovered. He found out that 60 percent of the two-year olds who had received very little touching, rocking and other forms of physical attention were delayed in many aspects of their motor development.

They also suffered a delay in the development of their emotions.

At the age of two, they could not sit unsupported, whereas the normal age for an infant to start sitting is six to seven months.

Studies on infants in Africa have shown that, in some areas, babies could sit as early as five months, crawl shortly thereafter and some of them even started walking at seven to eight months of age. The reason is that babies in those cultures are cuddled and carried close to the mother's skin and rocked and touched for about 18 hours a day. These children are strapped to their mother's bodies while they work in the fields and are in constant intimate physical contact with their mothers. All of this greatly enhances neuromuscular growth of the baby.

Human touch is the warmest and most loving of all touches. Babies who are hugged, touched and stroked are happy babies. They sleep better, feed better, gain weight faster, and tend to have better immunity compared with other babies who are deprived of the benefits of touch.

Babies who are stroked and touched regularly sit earlier, crawl earlier, stand earlier and walk earlier, because the touch sensation enhances the neuromuscular growth of the body.

Now that we know the importance and the benefits of touch, we should make sure that this vital sense is stimulated right from the time of birth.

Mothers and fathers today are encouraged to bond with the baby at birth by physically placing the undressed baby on their bare chest, and gently stroking and talking to the baby. This not only enhances the neuromuscular development of the child but also makes him emotionally more stable, happier and a well-bonded child.

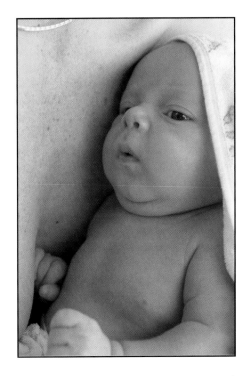

The sensation of touch also improves eye/hand coordination, and enhances large body movements such as walking and running.

It develops coordination of the smaller muscles of the body that are useful in skills such as painting, writing and other activities where hand and finger use is required.

Touching the skin of the newborn with different textures and shapes sharpens their ability to recognize various forms of surfaces.

Another very good and effective way to stimulate the sense of touch is to sit with your baby undressed in front of a large mirror.

Starting from the head, touch and name the various parts of his body such as the forehead, eyes, nose, chin and other body parts.

This play not only promotes the benefits of touch but it also serves as a source of information for the baby to know and recognize various parts of his body.

Early stimulation of the sense of touch will lead to children with sharper senses, brighter brains and a healthy body and mind.

* * * * * * * * * * * *

Chapter 7

Sensational Smell

Sensational Smell

At birth, vision and hearing are still not functioning to any great degree. Therefore, newborns have to rely much more on touch, taste, and smell in the initial stages of life.

In terms of importance, the sense of smell may rank lower down the order. However, for obvious reasons, newborns rely on this sense much more than other senses.

Let us have a look at how this entire sense of smell develops. After about five weeks of fertilization, a small pit appears on the primitive face, gradually deepening and dividing into two nostrils by the seventh week of gestation.

At about the same time, the specialized nerve cells called the olfactory epithelial cells start lining the nasal cavity.

By 11 weeks of gestation, the olfactory epithelial cells are quite mature and many in number. However, they do not actually begin to function until a few months later.

The ability to recognize odors and different smells begins around the 28th week of gestation and improves very rapidly from then onward.

A lot of people are surprised, when told that many odors that pregnant mothers are exposed to are also experienced by their fetuses inside the womb.

Infact, through the third trimester of pregnancy, a baby inside the womb smells almost everything the mother inhales, whether it is a pleasant or a repulsive odor.

The sense of smell is trapped by the olfactory epithelial cells lining the nostrils.

The sense of smell of the newborn plays a major role in building and strengthening the bond between the mother and the baby. It also instills emotional stability in the baby.

Through the nostrils, the message is carried by the olfactory nerve to the primary olfactory cortex or the smell sensing area of the brain, where all the information regarding the odor is processed.

As mentioned earlier, newborns tend to rely more on smell and the other less-important senses as opposed to vision and hearing.

This, of course, is for obvious reasons. The sense of smell does not require any special effort. Odors will travel through the air and reach the baby's nostrils from any corner of the room.

One of the most important functions of the sense of smell is to create bonding between the mother and the newborn.

Newborns are experts at recognizing the body odor of the mother and the odor of the mother's breast milk.

It is this perception of smell that helps the baby to locate the mother's breast and meet her nutritional needs.

Smell also plays a very important role in early emotional development, because through smell the bond between the parent and the baby is established.

A one-week-old baby can definitely tell the difference between the smell of their mother's breast milk compared to the milk of another woman.

The sense of smell is so unique that if the baby is presented with two cotton pads, one soaked in her mother's breast milk and the other soaked in another woman's milk, the baby will amazingly turn the head towards the cotton pad soaked in her mother's milk.

Sensational Smell

Since we know that the baby reacts to the odor of the mother, one of the good ways to promote and strengthen bonding between the two is to leave the mother's clothes that have been worn overnight in the baby's crib while she is resting or sleeping during the day.

In doing so, the baby is constantly being exposed to the odor of the mother, which leads to a sense of security in the baby and helps to build up her confidence.

Another good technique is to make the newborn smell cotton pads sprayed with Mom and Dad's regular perfume few times a day.

This helps the baby to identify their presence even when they are not close to her and promotes the bond of love, especially if the parents are away at work during a good part of the day.

Growing babies should be exposed to different smells all the time.

As babies grow up, they should be exposed to different smells all the time, which is very simple and easy to do. This can be achieved while doing almost any daily activity with the baby around, such as preparing food in the kitchen or bathing and changing the baby.

Newborn babies can distinguish between different odors. They manifest it by their facial expressions. They will turn their face toward a pleasant odor but turn away from any odor that is unpleasant.

It is therefore quite clear to us now that the perception of smell in a newborn helps in bonding, fostering a loving relationship with the parents and emotional stability.

Just like the other vital senses of vision, hearing, taste and touch, the more we stimulate the sense of smell the more connections we are forming between the nose and the brain.

Exposure to smells also has a great impact on other vital senses. A simple example is the connection between smell and the sense of taste which we experience every single day.

Smelling good food gives us watery mouths, and we can actually start tasting the food in our mouths even before we have started eating it.

Again, the critical period when nerve connections are building at a rapid rate is the best time to sharpen the skills of this vital sense.

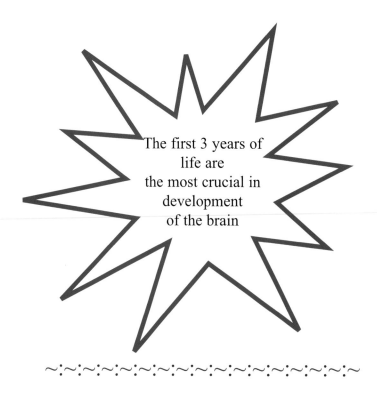

The first 3 years of life are the most crucial in development of the brain

~:~:~:~:~:~:~:~:~:~:~:~:~:~:~:~

Chapter 8

The joy of Taste

The Joy of Taste

The first taste buds in the mouth of the developing fetus emerge at about eight weeks after conception.

By the 13th week, taste buds are present throughout the mouth, on the surface of the tongue, palate and also the upper throat.

Taste buds mature by the end of the first trimester of pregnancy, which is just about the time when the fetus is beginning to show the sucking and swallowing reflexes. Once the sucking and the swallowing reflexes are established, the fetus starts to swallow the surrounding amniotic fluid.

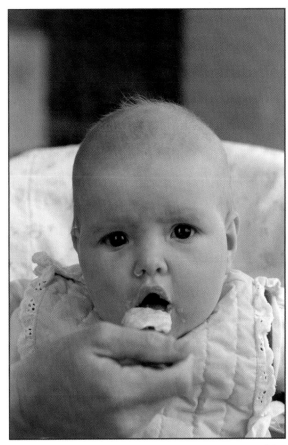

Chemical substances of various tastes, which are present in the amniotic fluid in the mother's womb, flow over the taste buds and stimulate them.

This stimulation of the taste buds helps to develop neural connections between the taste buds and the brain to recognize different tastes.

▽

The taste buds of a newborn can detect the four basic categories of tastes:

Sweet - Sour - Bitter - Salt.

The sense of taste integrates very closely with the sense of smell in appreciating different flavors of foods.

Taste buds are mostly distributed along the sides of the tongue, the tip and the back of the tongue, on the palate, sides of the mouth and the upper throat area.

Babies are born with a full set of 10,000 taste buds, which have the ability to differentiate between various tastes. However, it takes some years after birth before these taste buds are fully mature.

Babies prefer a sweet taste over a sour taste. Even a one-day-old baby will suck harder if offered a sweet drink as opposed to a sour drink.

Research indicates that the receptors for the sweet taste in taste buds, when stimulated, activate the release of endogenous opiates in the brain.

These natural opiates are morphine-like chemical substances that produce a sense of pleasure and well being.

Hence, it has been determined that there is a natural tendency in human beings to enjoy sweet taste.

Chapter 9

SPEECH AND LANGUAGE

SPEECH AND LANGUAGE

Researchers have long been intrigued by the questions: what is language and how does it evolve?

People from different parts of the world learn to speak and understand words at more or less the same age. They all follow similar stages of language development in their lives. This has led most researchers to believe that a baby's brain is pre-programmed to learn and acquire the art of language.

Language is made up of words, and words are made up of sounds. The basic sounds that make a language are called **phonemes.**

Phonemes differ from language to language. For example a phoneme in Chinese will be different from a **phoneme** in English.

English has a total of **40 phonemes.** There is clear evidence that babies even as young as two months of age can distinguish the different varieties of phonemes. It has also been found that **phonemes** are stored like sound tracks in the brain.

The human brain has the inbuilt property from the time of its formation to recognise and store different sounds.

Speech and Language

In early infancy, when the baby is only a few months old, he has the ability to perceive and record **phonemes** from many other languages, apart from the mother tongue.

After six months, babies tend to lose their grasp of phonemes of foreign languages. By one year of age, the ability for registering phonemes of another language other than their native language is gone.

By 12 months, babies lose the ability to discriminate sounds that are not significant in their native language.

Since babies perceive and grasp different kinds of phonemes, it is easier to teach them many different languages at the same time.

The reason most adults have more difficulty in learning and speaking foreign languages is because the ability to recognize phonemes of a foreign language has been lost after the age of one year.

However, due to the elasticity of the brain, babies are still able to grasp a foreign language quite well during their critical period of brain growth, the first three years of life.

Babies learn to talk by listening to the language spoken around them. The more words they hear, the faster they learn to talk, and the bigger their vocabulary becomes.

It is not only the amount of language they are exposed to, that is important, but also the way in which the speaker interacts with the baby. According to research by Dr. Janellen Huttenlocher, the actual size of a toddler's vocabulary is directly related to the amount of communication between the mother and the baby.

At 20 months of age the children of chatty mothers averaged 131 more words than the children of mothers who did not speak much to their babies.
In the same group, at two years of age, the gap had increased to about 295 words. This proves that communication, and the quality of language that babies are exposed to, is vital for the development of vocabulary and language.

According to a finding of the MacArthur Communicative Development Inventories (CDIs), an average 12-month-old baby understands around 55 words but may speak only one or two words, and an average 16-month-old understands about 170 words and can say only about 25.

It is not only the vocabulary and the amount of language, but children who have been exposed to good quality language tend to be more intelligent and have shown to score higher on IQ tests even as early as five years of age.

Language is the means of expressing our thought processes. It is a window of communication between an individual and the outside world. It is important to develop language in order to communicate how we feel and think in our minds and to know how others feel and think.

The importance of being able to express one's self and be understood is very evident in young toddlers. In early stages when they are still unable to speak and express themselves, though their thought process is maturing very quickly, the frustration of not being able to express themselves and be understood is the reason for temper tantrums.

The development of language, and how it is acquired in small children, is a fairly predictable path. Children may not acquire the same characteristics of language at exactly the same times, but almost all children acquire the art of language in roughly the same order and pattern.

A language explosion starts at about 18 months of age when a child has a spoken vocabulary of roughly 50 words and understands about 200 words. By the time the baby is 24 months old, the vocabulary is over 200 words of spoken language and an understanding of as many as 1,000 words or more.

After two years of age, it is difficult to keep track of the growth and diversity of the language, because of the increased interaction of the child with the outside world.

Of course, it will vary from child to child, depending on the interaction, the quality and the quantity of the language that has been offered by the parents and other caregivers.

ℴ At about two months, babies start to produce cooing sounds. These are the first sounds a baby makes when happy or excited.
ℴ At about four months, they will start to produce growling and bubbling sounds. At this stage, babies love to yell, laugh, squeal and make gooing sounds.

Babbling usually begins at six months. All babies make the same kinds of sounds, no matter what their background or race or what their native language is.

Speech and Language

Even deaf babies babble. When a baby is cooing, or babbling the parents or the care givers should reciprocate in the same manner. This encourages the baby to learn how to communicate and helps greatly in acquiring early language skills.

Development of language and its relationship to babbling has always been a matter of debate. However it is reasonable to assume, that babbling is a good preliminary exercise to gain control of the tongue, lips, and palate, which are the essential organs for producing sounds and language.

Between six and nine months of age, babies have more control over the sounds they make and the syllables they produce. They can also make echoing sounds such as 'babababa' or 'dadadada.' Many times, this is taken by the parents as the first word that the baby has uttered, which is actually not true. In any case, it is exciting for the parents, and encourages them to put more stress on the development of language skills of their baby Toward the end of the first year, babies can put a few sounds together and make them sound purposeful, especially when reaching out to grab something or asking for an object, food or toy.

A delay in language development is the most common childhood disability

This is the first form of communication which of course begins long before proper meaningful words will be uttered.

The brain expresses thoughts in the form of language. Proper language development is therefore very important. A delay in language development is the most common childhood disability, affecting up to 10 percent or more of all seven-year old. Imprinting the brain by exposure to intense, intelligent and high-quality language is therefore very critical in the first year of life and especially in the first six months.

Motherese is a very effective way of starting communication with the baby

The importance of how to communicate with babies and the manner in which we speak to babies and address them is extremely important in developing the quality of the language that the child will eventually acquire.

The first form of language between child and mother is called "Motherese."

therese is the musical type of language with a special rhythm and ch that the mother uses when talking to a small baby. The pitch goes up and down more often than in a normal speech pattern. When we use motherese, we speak slower and also use shorter sentences. Motherese is an effective way to start communication with the baby. It is simple for the baby to understand and is musical to the baby's ears. It may not necessarily be grammatically correct all the time, but it helps the baby to become an active participant in the conversation process and gives the baby a lot of confidence. Motherese helps to promote love, affection and bonding between the mother and the baby. It is also very helpful in the emotional development of the child.

The essence of communication, speech and language development has three important pillars

* THE COMMUNICATION TECHNIQUE

* QUALITY OF COMMUNICATION

* OPPORTUNITIES FOR LANGUAGE INTERACTION

* THE COMMUNICATION TECHNIQUE

Communication is an act of receiving and relaying information. It is an exercise where equal participation is required from both parties.

The basic rule is that although your baby may not be able to express herself in spoken language, it is important to ensure that you are participating in her cooing, babbling and squealing.

When she coos or babbles, reciprocate in the same manner varying the tone and pitch of your voice.

When having a conversation with the baby, look at her face and eyes, keeping yourself within her visual field. Look at the baby attentively and talk slowly. Use small sentences and clear language.

The tone of the caregiver's voice is important and conveys a lot of meaningful expressions. When talking to the baby, the tone should be soft and loving.

Before starting a conversations you must determine the mood and the state of the baby's mind. It is useless to make conversation when the baby is hungry, irritable or crying.

Some of the most important prerequisites for communication are your facial expressions, the eye movements, movements of the mouth and lips and the overall body language. This acts like icing on the cake in developing the child's communication skills.

Personal interaction with the baby is essential to stimulate the development of language. This is why babies will not benefit by sitting in front of television sets for endless hours. Exposing the baby to television lacks personal interaction and also lacks control over the quality and the relevance of language for the baby. Television viewing for small babies should be discreetly monitored, and babies and young children should be exposed to proper educational and informative programs.

When the baby reaches the age that you have started to use 'Motherese' more often, the way you express things should be modified and changed.

You must use sentences which are more like questions rather than statements.

For example:

'Would you like to take a bath now?'
'Would you like your cereal now?'
'Would you like to go for a walk?'
'Would you like to go to bed?'

Talking to the baby in this manner enhances their participation, instills self confidence in the baby and is beneficial for their emotional development.

* QUALITY OF COMMUNICATION

The contents of the language, the descriptive manner, the rhythm and the continuity in the language are extremely important. Let us take an example of a mother playing with her baby. An example of good quality conservation would be:

---

* Hi Sam. Look at these balloons! Do you like these balloons?
This is a big balloon.
This is a bigger balloon! This balloon is small! Here, look at this red balloon.
Would you like to touch the blue balloon? Oh, that balloon went up in the sky!
Can you see where it has gone? See how it goes up!

This way, you will not only converse with the baby but also get him to participate in the activity. Discussing the size, the shape, the color and the movements of the balloon not only provides interesting conversation with baby, but it also gives the baby intelligent information.

OPPORTUNITIES FOR LANGUAGE

An intelligent parent will use any available opportunity and time to communicate with the baby. These windows of opportunities are limitless and are freely available in our daily lives. Maximum advantage should be taken while:

Feeding the baby.

Bathing and changing the baby.

Taking the baby out for a walk.

Playing with the baby.

A trip to the grocery store.

A trip to the park.

These are just a few examples of how broad our horizon of communication with the baby is. In each of these situations, use the tips that we discussed in the paragraph on "Quality of Communication." Be as descriptive as possible in terms of objects, situations, actions and their meanings, and the objectives of your actions.

Speech and Language

Remember, the more information you give your baby, the more language you are using and the bigger the base you are providing for her vocabulary and intelligence.

Story telling, singing nursery rhymes and lullabies and, last but not least, reading storybooks are all very effective tools in promoting development of language.

All infant educators are unanimous in their views on the importance and benefits of an early introduction to reading.

It may sound difficult, but if you place your three-month-old baby in your lap and hold a colorful storybook in front of her, you are sure to get her attention and concentration. This not only exposes the baby to vocabulary, but by reading we are also stimulating the other important vital senses of the baby. While reading a book, the infant not only sees colors, shapes, numbers, letters and pictures, but also benefits from the experience of continuity of language which accompanies story reading.

Babies are born pre-programmed to acquire languages. Nurturing this ability, by intelligent parenting and a healthy social environment, will determine the eventual outcome of this important talent.
Remember, good language skills will also stimulate the development of the other vital senses.

Chapter 10

Masyog
(Massage & yoga)

Masyog

Masyog is a combination of massage and yoga. Massage speeds up motor development. The sooner the baby starts with motor development and gross motor movements, the earlier he will start to perceive the world around him. Early motor development not only helps the baby sit or crawl at an earlier age, but also speeds up the entire range of his developing milestones. Massage and yoga increase muscle power and make the joints stronger and more flexible.

Massage and yoga develop bonding and increase emotional and physical attachment between mother and baby. Babies who are massaged regularly are more relaxed and happier. They have a better sleeping pattern, a healthier appetite, gain weight faster and are less agitated.

In some parts of the Eastern world, it has been a tradition for centuries for the baby to be massaged with oil, followed by stretches and a warm bath. It is best to start with massage and then go on to yoga stretches, both of which are described in detail later in this chapter.

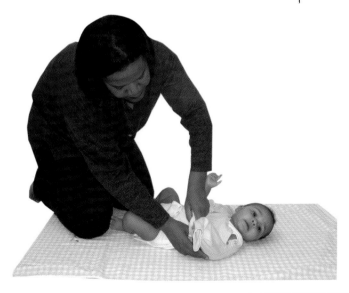

a stretches are very relaxing, and relaxation plays an important role e development of emotions and the nervous system. While giving the baby a massage and doing the yoga stretches, we are also stimulating his other vital senses such as vision, smell, language and balance.

There are no hard-and-fast rules regarding the time and place for Masyog. It can be practised at the convenience of you and the baby. It could be a mid-morning, mid-afternoon or even a mid-evening session. Make sure that the place is warm and cozy. A soft mattress should be placed on the floor, preferably in the center of the room, away from sharp objects or edges. Any kind of oil, for example baby oil, lavender oil or olive oil, can be used.

Both you and the baby should be completely relaxed and happy. You should squat on the floor, with your knees in a flexed position. Take a few slow and deep breaths to relieve your mind of all anxieties and worries. Relax your body muscles, especially the neck and shoulders.

Lay the baby on his back on the mattress. Place your right hand in a loving manner across the baby's chest. This will relax the baby and establish contact between you and the baby.

The next step is by far the most important step. You must take permission from the baby before beginning Masyog. This can be done by talking to the baby gently and lovingly. Establish eye-to-eye contact while gently rubbing the chest of the baby in circular motions. This ensures that the baby is comfortable and happy before the Masyog begins.

Just before beginning Masyog, put a few drops of oil on both palms and rub them gently together to lubricate and warm your hands.

> **Caution:**
>
> I would like to stress that concerns for safety are extremely important in any manoeuvre involving physical handling of the baby, especially if the baby has a medical condition. Please seek the advice of your doctor before starting any kind of physical exercise for the baby.

MASSAGE ROUTINES

Starting the massage from the front of the body is always a good idea. This establishes eye-to-eye contact and language communication with the baby. It keeps the baby relaxed and makes the whole exercise more enjoyable for yourself and the baby.

Upper Body Strokes:

1. **Cross strokes on the chest:** Place your right hand at the lower level of the baby's rib cage on the right side. With a gentle sweeping action, glide your hand across the chest toward the left shoulder and finish the movement by holding the shoulder and the shoulder joint in your palm. Repeat three times and carry on the same movement now with your left hand placed on the left side of the baby's chest.

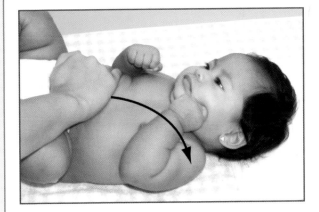

2. Oval strokes on the chest: Place both hands on the center of the baby's lower rib cage and, with gentle gliding movements, go up to the neck and out toward the shoulders. Glide your hands down to the lower rib cage and back toward the center of the chest. Repeat three times, ending the final movement with a stroke at the shoulder.

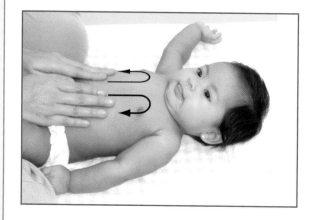

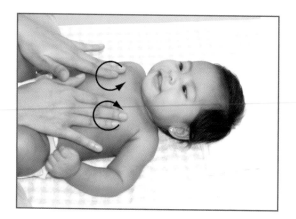

3. Circular strokes: Place the first three fingers of your hands on the chest with the middle finger making contact with the baby's nipple.
Stroke simultaneously in a circular fashion from inside out. Repeat this movement a few times.

4. Massaging the arms: Place the palms of your hands on the baby's shoulders and gently massage a few times in a circular motion. Then massage the arms individually, starting at the shoulder and going downward to the wrist.

Holding the baby's arm between your thumbs and the index fingers move in circular motion in opposite directions, starting from the top of the arm toward the wrist using gentle pressure. Open and close the elbow joint a few times.

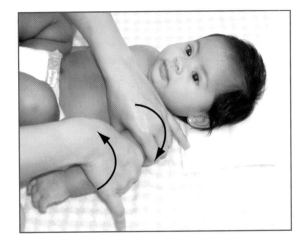

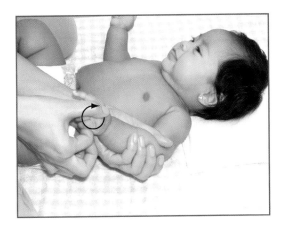

5. Massaging the hands: Use one hand to support the wrist of the baby and hold the palm with the other. Starting at the outer surface of the wrist and using your thumb and index finger make gentle circular movements going downward toward the fingers. Repeat the same circular movements and massage the palm of the baby. Open the hand and massage the tips of the fingers in a circular motion with your thumb and index finger. Give a very gentle tug to each finger and finish off the massage.

6. Final strokes of the arms.: Finish off the arm massage with the popular Indian Milking Action. Encircle the top of the baby's arm with your hands and slide downward toward the wrist in a milking action. Repeat a few times and perform the same action for the other arm. Make sure that your hands are lubricated with massaging oil.

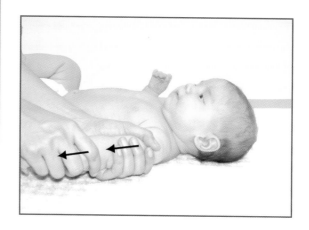

TUMMY MASSAGE

Tummy massage is very relaxing for babies. It relieves them of flatulence and also improves their digestion. Babies who get tummy massage regularly seem to feed better and also have less colic..

1. Cross Strokes of the tummy: Place your right hand just above the baby's right hip joint. With a gentle flowing movement glide toward the left lower part of the baby's ribcage. Now gently bring your hand downward, finishing off by stroking the outer part of the baby's abdomen. Repeat the same with your left hand placed above the left hip joint of the baby.

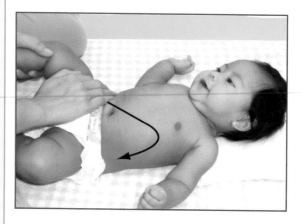

2. Downward strokes across tummy: Place one of your hands on the upper part of the baby's tummy just under the ribcage and gently glide downward toward the groin. While this hand is crossing over the umbilical area, place the other hand under the ribcage at the point where this movement was begun. Using both hands, carry out the continuous strokes a few times.

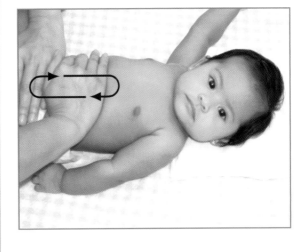

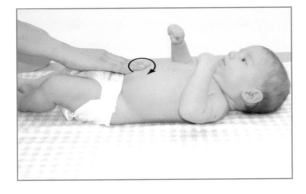

3. Circular strokes: Place the first three fingers of your hand over the umbilical area of the baby and gently start with circular movements. Keep expanding the circle going outward toward the abdominal edges. As the circle expands, use your palm to cover the entire area of the baby's abdomen.

LOWER BODY MASSAGE

Ensure that the baby is in a comfortable position. Place both hands around the baby's hips and gently stroke down both legs, ending the movement at the soles of the feet and the toes.

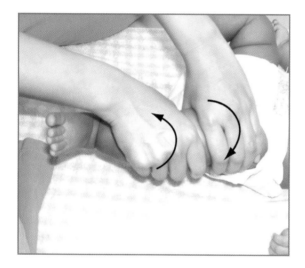

1. Massaging the legs: Place both hands on the hip joint. Move the hands in opposite directions and use a gliding action from the top of the leg to the ankle. Make sure to apply gentle pressure on the legs. Repeat this movement a few times and finish off by opening and closing the knee joint a few times. Repeat the same movements on the other leg.

Masyog helps to achieve motor skills early

2. Massaging the feet: Place one hand around the baby's ankle. Start the massage with the thumb and index finger of your other hand, begin with small circular movements on either side of the baby's ankle. Move the baby's ankle joint gently in a clockwise and counterclockwise direction a few times.

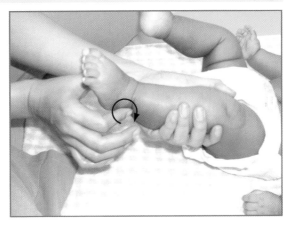

Also move the foot up and down at the ankle a few times. Using the index and middle finger, stroke the top of the foot from the ankle toward the toes.

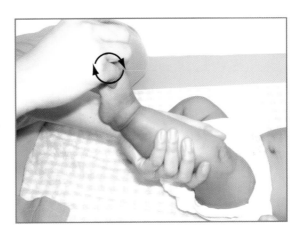

Elevate the foot slightly, still holding at the ankle. Using the thumb, start off with small circular movements at the center of the sole of the foot extending toward the periphery.

With your thumb, stroke the outer and the inner edge of the foot a few times, and finish off by gently pulling on each toe.

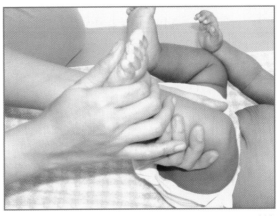

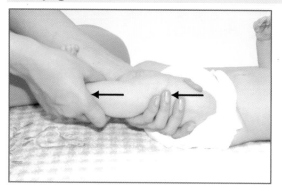

3. Final stroke for the legs: Using the same ever-popular Indian Milking Stroke, start from the thigh down toward the baby's foot. Ensure that the hands are well lubricated.

BACK MASSAGE

Massage the baby's back with the baby lying comfortably face down on the floor or across your thighs. Since there is no eye contact with the baby in this position, it is very important to keep talking and reassuring the baby.

1. Cross strokes of the back: Place your right hand just above the baby's left hip joint and glide it smoothly and gently toward the baby's right shoulder. Repeat the same movement from the right hip joint with your left hand. Repeat the routine a few times.

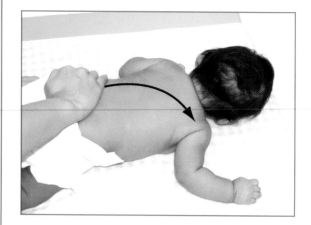

2. Strokes of the shoulder blades: Place the palms of both your hands on either side of the baby's spine at the shoulder blade level, and start off with gentle circular movements going from the center toward the periphery.

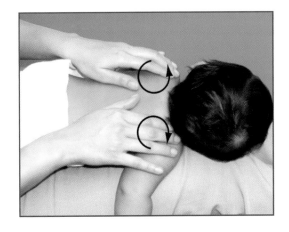

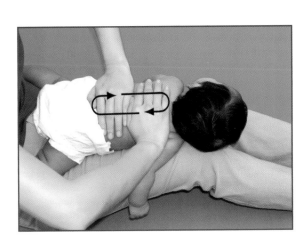

3. Downward strokes of the back: Place one hand across the shoulder blades of the baby. Starting at just under the neck, glide the hand downward toward the bottom. Once you are midway down the back, place the other hand at the top so that using both hands, it becomes a continuous top-to-bottom movement. Repeat a few times, ending off at the base of the spine.

At this point, apply gentle pressure on the lower part of the spine and carry out small circular clockwise and counterclockwise movements.

4. Strokes on the spine and on the sides: Place your thumb on the upper part of baby's spine, just under the neck. Glide the thumb over the spine from the top to the bottom. Apply gentle pressure throughout this movement. Repeat a few times. On the final stroke use the thumb for small circular movements at the tail bone.

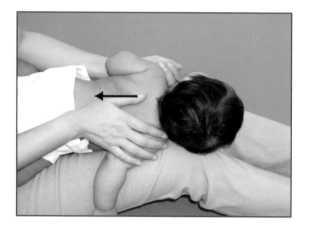

5. Place the fingers of both hands at the base of the neck on either side of the baby's spine. Start with gentle circular movements from the top to the bottom. As you keep repeating this movement, increase the size of the circular movements to cover the entire back from the center toward the periphery.

6. Strokes for the legs: With the baby still lying in the face-down position, place both hands on the baby's legs just under the buttocks. Move both hands in opposite directions and with gentle pressure glide down toward the ankle. Repeat a few times. Finish off the stroke by massaging the tendon just above the heel of the foot.

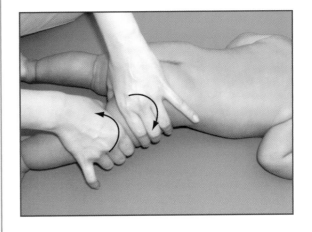

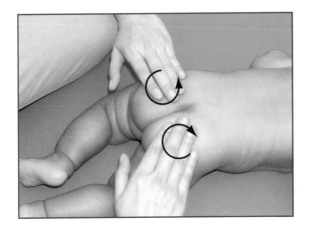

7. Strokes for the buttocks. Place the fingers of your hands on each buttock and apply gentle regular pressure on the buttocks. Start with circular movements from the center extending outward. Finish off by opening and closing the buttocks a few times.

HEAD, NECK AND FACE MASSAGE

Lay the baby comfortably on his back. Make eye contact with the baby and keep talking to him.

1. Head stroke: Place your hand across the baby's forehead and glide it stroking the head all the way down to the neck. This is very soothing and comforting for the baby.

2. Neck stroke: Place the first three fingers of your hands on either side of the baby's neck at the shoulder and massage with gentle circular motions. Glide your hands on the sides and the back of the neck, finishing off with gentle circular motions toward the spine. Hold the baby's face in both hands and gently move the face from side to side.

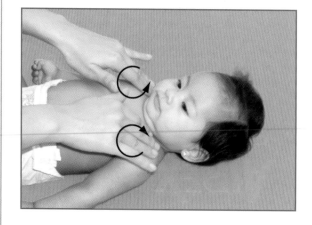

3. Face strokes: Place your thumbs at the center of the forehead and gently glide down toward the temple on either side. Make sure to apply gentle pressure during this manoeuvre and finish off with circular movements at both temples. After that, place both thumbs at the center of the eyebrows and stretch the eyebrows by moving the thumbs from the center toward the temples.

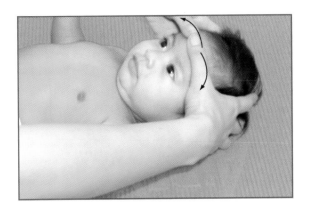

Having finished with the forehead, hold the bridge of the nose at eye level between your thumb and the index finger and massage gently in a circular manner. Place both thumbs on either side of the nostrils and glide them toward the temples, exerting gentle pressure and stretching at the same time.

Place both thumbs on the upper lip, one under each nostril, and stretch outward toward the angle of the mouth. Starting at the same point again, extend this movement from the nostrils backward toward the ear lobes.

Place both thumbs on the chin and glide them along the jaw bone up toward the earlobes. Hold the chin between your thumb and index finger and tickle a few times.

Hold the ears between the thumb and the index finger and massage gently from top to bottom. End this stroke by holding the earlobes and massaging them gently.

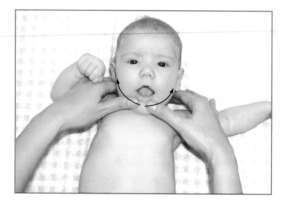
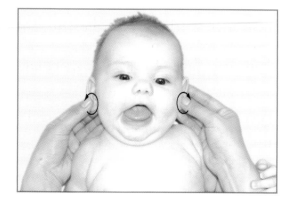

YOGA STRETCHES

YOGA STRETCHES

IN THE FIRST & SECOND MONTH:

Once you have completed massaging the baby, you can proceed on to the next step of Masyog which is Yoga Stretches.

Yoga is practiced by millions of people. Especially in the East, yoga is considered a wonderful way of relaxing and improving the health of the body, mind and soul.

A baby's muscles are warm after the Massage Routines, and therefore this is the best time to continue with the Yoga Stretches.

The principle here remains the same. Both you and the baby should be totally relaxed.

Visual and vocal contact between you and the baby is of immense importance.

Take a few deep breaths, inhaling and exhaling slowly with your eyes closed. It is recommended that you do a few stretches of your upper and lower body so that your muscles are totally relaxed and you are ready to handle the baby.

Sit upright with your legs crossed under you and with your back as straight as possible. Place your hand on your baby's chest and move it in a circular clockwise manner slowly and gently a few times. Repeat the same stroke with your hand on the baby's abdomen.

With the baby lying on his back, place your hand on the baby's forehead and gently glide across the head going down toward the neck.

Carry on this movement by using both hands and gliding down from the base of the neck along the spine, gently stroking the bottom. Continue along the back of the thighs and the legs down to the soles of the feet. End up with gentle circular motions at the soles of the feet.

With babies up to two-months old, handle the upper half of the baby's body very gently. The head and neck of the baby are still not stable. Let us start with the stretches from the lower half of the body going upward.

LOWER BODY STRETCHES

1. FEET STRETCHES – With the baby lying relaxed on his back in front of you, place one hand on both knees. Firmly place the palm of the other hand flat against the feet of the baby. Move the feet in a rhythmical pattern up and down a few times.

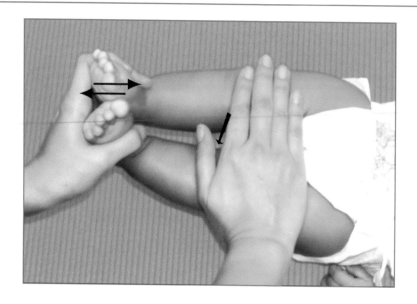

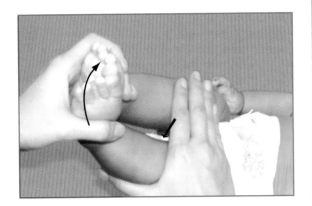

2: LEG STRETCHES

Hold the baby's ankles with one hand and place the other hand on the knees. Raise the ankles, keeping the legs straight at the knees. Keep raising till the soles of the feet point toward the ceiling. Hold for a count of five, relax and bring the feet to the original position. Repeat this stretch a few times.

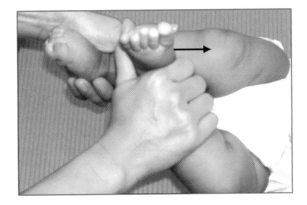

3. In the next movement, hold the baby's left ankle in your right hand. Glide the left heel over the right shin bringing it to knee level. Hold and press toward the groin. Repeat the same manoeuvre with the right heel gliding on the left shin, going up toward the left knee and finish off by again pressing toward the groin.

HIP AND PELVIC STRETCHES

1. Hold the upper part of the legs around the knee. Open the legs slightly wider than the hips, and press both knees against the abdomen, going as much toward the ribcage as possible. Release and repeat a few times.

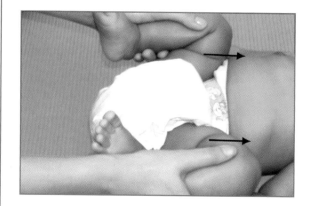

2. Gently flex the legs at the knees. Bring both knees together and move from the midline to the right to an angle of about 45 degrees. Bring the knees back to midline. Move to the same angle on the left side, again coming back to the midline. Repeat the entire sequence a few times.

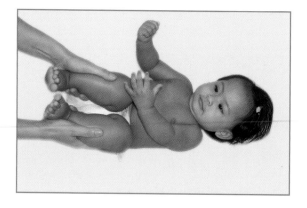

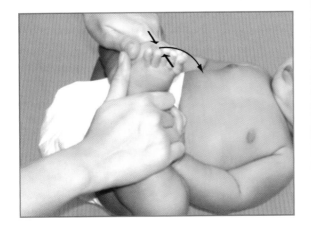

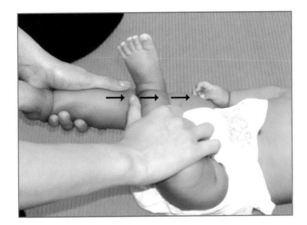

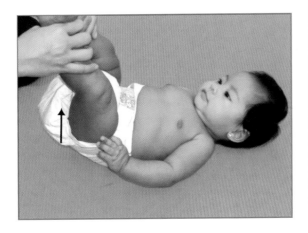

3. Hold the soles of the baby's feet against one another in the midline, and push them toward the groin as much as possible. Release pressure and repeat the movement a few times.

4. Place baby's left heel on his right knee and gently move the heel toward the baby's right hip. Try to go as high as is comfortable for the baby. Repeat the same on the opposite side.

5. Hold both the baby's ankles together with the knees flexed. Draw the ankles gently toward her chest. Repeat a few times. On the final movement, hold the baby's leg straight, raise them toward the ceiling till the baby's bottom is clear off the floor. Repeat a few times and gently let her bottom rest on the floor.

UPPER BODY STRETCHES

ARM STRETCHES:

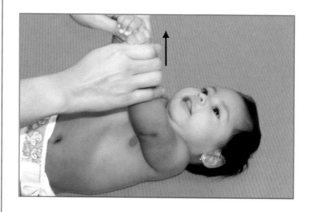

1. Place the baby comfortably on his back on the mattress, Hold him by both his wrists. Bring both wrists in the midline in front of the face. Pull gently to give sufficient stretch to the arms and shoulder blades.

2. Stretch baby's arms to the sides in line with the shoulders. Hold the baby's left wrist in your left hand and the baby's right wrist in your right. Cross the wrists toward the opposite shoulder, going as far as the baby will allow. Repeat a few times.

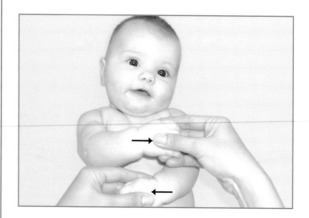

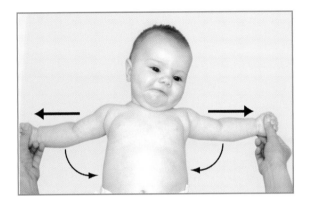

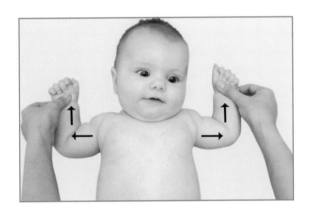

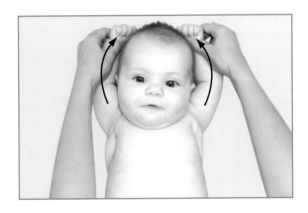

3. Stretch the baby's arms to the sides in line with the shoulders. Bring one hand at a time close to the body then go back to the original position. Repeat with both hands touching the sides of the body and going back to the original position together.

4. Start with the arms flexed at the elbows so that the baby's wrists are in line with the ears. Gently move one arm toward the head, going as far as possible. Repeat a few times on both sides. Finally repeat the manoeuvre with both arms going upward toward the head at the same time.

5. Hold baby's arms in the mid-line in front of face with both wrists placed against each other. Pull gently and move from the mid-line to 45 degrees on the right, come back to the mid-line and then move to the left. Repeat a few times on both sides.

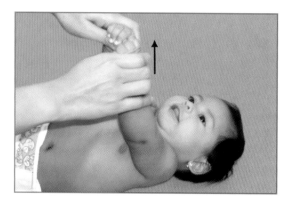
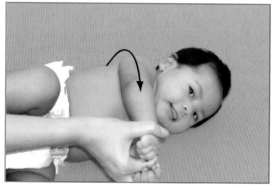

YOGA STRETCHES
(THIRD MONTH ONWARD)

In the first two months, the baby's muscle tone is not very well developed and there is limited head and neck control. The yoga stretches of the upper body therefore have been very gentle.

By the third month, however, the baby is bigger and there is better head and neck control. We can now start with more elaborate stretches of the upper body, the back and the spine.

We can now also increase the range of stretches for the lower body.

LOWER BODY STRETCHES (Third month)

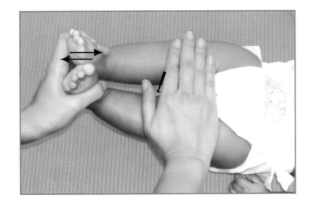

1. FEET STRETCHES- With the baby lying relaxed on her back, place one hand on both the knees and push gently toward the floor. Firmly place the palm of the other hand flat against the feet of the baby. Move the feet in a rhythmical pattern up and down a few times.

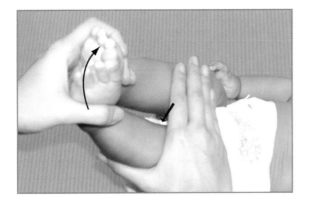

2. LEG STRETCHES - Hold baby's ankles with one and place the other hand on the knees. Raise the ankles, keeping the legs straight at the knees. Keep raising till the soles of the feet point toward the ceiling. Hold for a count of five, then relax and bring the feet to the original position. Repeat this stretch a few times.

3. Hold both of the baby's ankles. Glide the left heel over the right shin, bringing it to the knee level. Hold and press toward the groin. Repeat the same manoeuvre with the right heel gliding on the left shin toward the left knee.

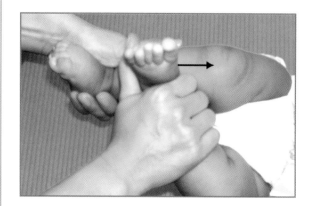

HIP AND PELVIC STRETCHES (Third month)

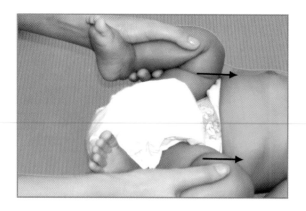

1. Hold the upper part of the baby's legs at the level of the knee joint. Open them slightly wider than the hips and press both knees against the abdomen, going as much toward the ribcage as possible. Release and repeat a few times.

2. Hold the soles of the baby's feet against one another in the midline and push them toward the groin as much as possible. Release pressure and repeat the movement a few times.

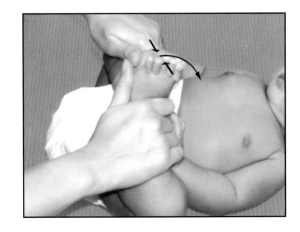

3. Place the left heel of the baby on his right knee, and gently move the heel toward the baby's right hip. By now, the baby is used to this stretch, and the muscles and the joints are more flexible and relaxed. With time, it will be possible to stretch the heel as far as the armpit or even the face. We have so often seen that babies enjoy pulling their feet and putting them in their mouth.

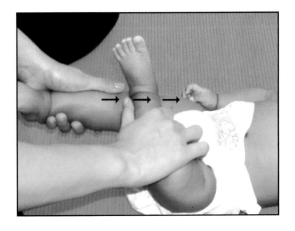

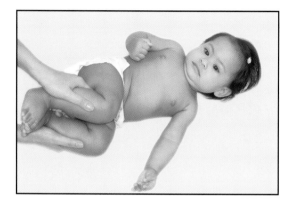

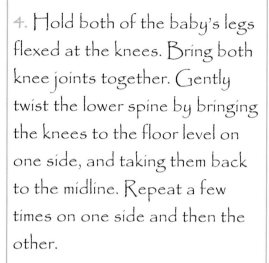

4. Hold both of the baby's legs flexed at the knees. Bring both knee joints together. Gently twist the lower spine by bringing the knees to the floor level on one side, and taking them back to the midline. Repeat a few times on one side and then the other.

5. Hold both the baby's ankles together with the knees flexed. Draw the ankles gently toward the chest. Repeat a few times. On the final movement, hold the baby's legs straight and raise them toward the ceiling till the baby's bottom and lower back are raised off the floor and only the shoulders are on the ground. Repeat a few times, gently letting the bottom rest on the floor.

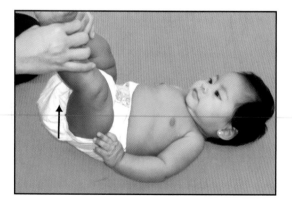

UPPER BODY STRETCHES (Third month)

ARM STRETCHES

1. Place the baby comfortably on her back. Hold him by the wrists. Bring both wrists in the midline in front of the face. Pull gently to give sufficient stretch to the arms and the shoulder blades by clearing the head and the shoulder blades from the floor.

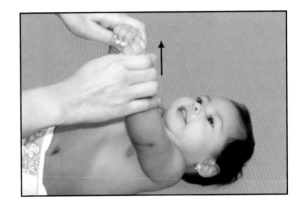

2. Hold the baby's wrists in the same position in front and in midline over the face. Start with circular movements at the shoulder joints in a clockwise manner first, then repeat the same movement in a counter clockwise direction.

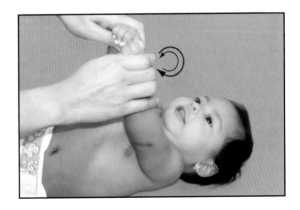

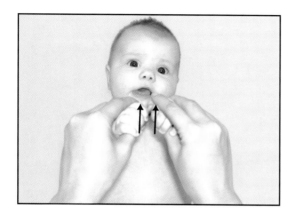

3. Hold the baby's hands with your thumb against the palms. Help the baby sit up from a lying down position, then on to a standing position. Gently lay the baby back on the floor. Repeat a few times.

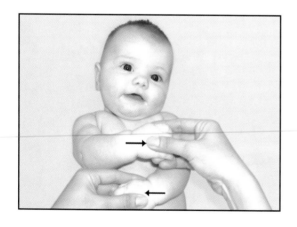

4. Stretch the baby's arms to the sides in line with the shoulders. Hold the baby's left wrist in your right hand, and the baby's right wrist in your left. Cross the wrists over to the opposite shoulder and keep going till the hands touch the opposite shoulder. Repeat a few times.

5. Stretch the baby's arms to the sides in line with the shoulders. Bring one hand at a time close to the body, going back to the original position. Repeat with both hands touching the sides of the body, then go back to the original position in line with his shoulders.

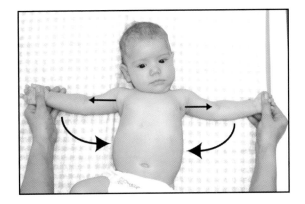

6. Start with the baby's arms stretched out. Keep the arms flexed at the elbows so that the wrists are in line with the ears. Gently move one arm toward the head, going as far as possible. Repeat a few times and do the same for the other side. Finally, repeat the manoeuvre with both arms going upward toward the center of the head. Try touching the fingers of both hands over the baby's head.

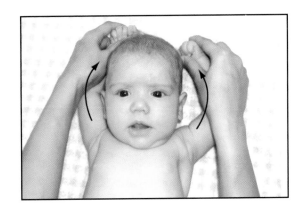

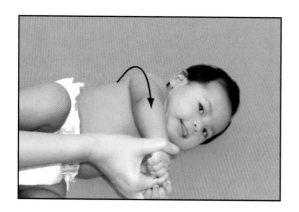

7. Hold the baby's arms in the midline and in front of his face with both wrists placed against each other. Pull gently and move from the midline to the right. Roll the baby over till the wrists touch the floor. Bring back to the midline. Repeat a few times and do the same stretch in the opposite direction.

BACK AND SPINAL STRETCHES (in the third month)

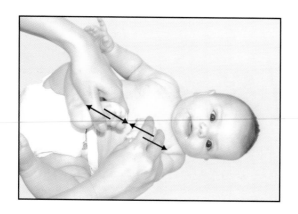

1. With the baby lying comfortably on his back, hold one arm at the wrist with one hand, and the opposite ankle of the baby with your other hand. First, stretch the arm upward and the leg downward diagonally.

Next, bring the wrist and the ankle together in front and in the midline of the baby. Open and close a few times. Repeat the same manoeuvre on the opposite side.

2. Hold the baby's right hand with your left and his left ankle with your right. Bring them to the midline. Move them gently in clockwise and counterclockwise rotations a few times. Repeat the same with the other arm and leg.

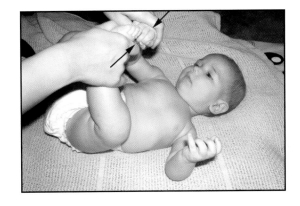

3. With the baby's wrist and the opposite ankle held in the midline, cross over with the ankle going toward the baby's shoulder and the wrist going toward the baby's hip. Stretch as far as possible. Repeat the same on the opposite side.

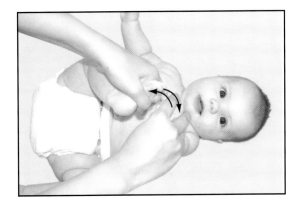

4. Place the baby face down, lying comfortably on your thighs. Slide both your palms under the arms toward the baby's chest. Lift the chest upward and downward a few times.

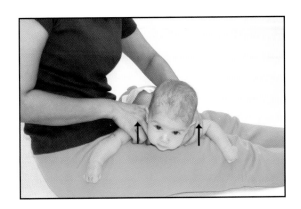

5. Place one hand under the baby's chest and the other at the lower end of the spine. Raise the chest and press the spine. Repeat a few times.

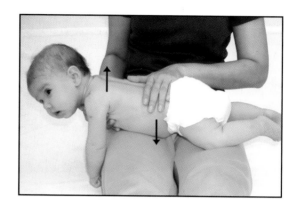

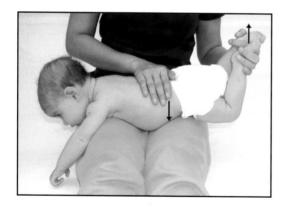

6. Place one hand on the lower part of the baby's spine just above the buttocks. With the other hand, hold his ankles. Raise the ankles, and at the same time, apply gentle pressure on the spine. Repeat a few times.

Chapter 10

BALANCING
And
ROCKING

BALANCING and ROCKING

The human ear is comprised of three parts:

> The outer ear ~ The middle ear ~ The inner ear.

Inside the inner ear are lodged the vestibular organ and the cochlea, which is the hearing apparatus.

The vestibular organ helps us to detect:

* The way the head turns during its movements.
* **Our body movement in linear planes.**
* Head tilt and the overall position of the body with respect to gravity.

Once these movements of the body have been detected by the vestibular organ, they are then conveyed through the vestibular nerve to the brain.

From the brain, the information about the balance and the motion of the body is relayed to the eye and to the neurons in the spinal cord that control the position of the arms and the legs and the overall posture of the body. This message is also relayed to the cerebellum.

The cerebellum is the part of the brain that is lodged at the back of the skull and lies adjacent to the brain stem. The main function of the cerebellum is to help in maintaining balance and coordination of body movements.

Vestibular Stimulation enhances the motor skills of an infant

Balancing and Rocking

It is therefore understandable that the cerebellum grows at a very rapid rate in the first year of life

It is during the first year of life that the infant transforms from an immobile person to one who has rapidly learned to crawl, stand and walk. All these activities, of course, require a sharp sense of balance.

The cerebellum integrates vestibular information with the senses of vision and touch. Altogether, they act to coordinate the sense of balance of the body.

The importance of the vestibular apparatus can be illustrated by the fact that the vestibular nerve is the first nerve in the entire brain to begin myelinating. This starts at around the last week of the first trimester of pregnancy.

By the fifth month of gestation, the vestibular apparatus has reached its full size and shape. Early maturity of the vestibular system is important, because this is what allows the fetus to sense his position in the womb with respect to gravity.

Vestibular stimulation has a marked effect on the motor skills of the infant. Infants who receive vestibular stimulation will start to have early and good control of the head, shoulders and back muscles. They will crawl early, sit unsupported early, and eventually stand and walk earlier than normal. Early development of motor skills helps the baby to explore her surroundings with more ease and interest. It enhances the development of other important vital senses as well.

Vestibular stimulation has a very positive effect on the development of a child's emotional and cognitive abilities.

The cerebellum maintains balance & coordination of the body movements.

Techniques for the Stimulation of the Vestibular Apparatus

Vestibular stimulation is carried out by holding the baby in a comfortable position and moving her body in different directions.

> Caution:-
> During any manoeuvre that involves the physical handling of the baby, safety is of paramount importance. If your baby has a medical condition, seek the advice of your doctor before proceeding with any form of physical exercise.
> Make sure that you and the baby are in a relaxed state of body and mind before carrying out these movements. The movements should be performed very smoothly. Jerky movements can cause physical harm to the baby.

The stimulation techniques also provide a lot of fun for the parents as well as the babies.

Following are some of the effective techniques:

UPWARD AND DOWNWARD MOVEMENTS.

✳ Standing in an upright position, hold the baby under the arms and bring her to your face level. Raise her over your head, bringing her back into the original position in one swift movement.

✳ Starting from the eye level again, bend yourself at the knees and move the baby downward, coming back to the original position in one swift motion. Repeat both routines a few times.

BACKWARD AND FORWARD MOVEMENT

✳ Standing with your feet wide apart, bend forward and hold the baby under the arms. Now gently swing her backward and forward between your legs. Repeat a few times.

SIDEWAY SWINGS

✳ Stand upright, holding the baby under the arms with your hands outstretched. Move the baby sideways in both directions. Repeat a few times.

HALF CIRCLE SWINGS

✳ Stand upright with your feet wide apart, gripping the baby under the arms. Swing the baby on either side in half circles.

ROCKING TO AND FRO

✳ Place the baby face down on your forearms flat against her tummy and rock gently from left to right and vice versa.

SPINNING

✳ Spinning is a very good means of vestibular stimulation and will help in early achievement of motor milestones. An easy and effective way of spinning is to sit with the baby in a revolving chair and spin gently in either direction.

BALANCING

✳ Sit the baby on your knees facing away from you. Place both the baby's palms against your palms and help the baby balance.

HEAD DOWN POSITION

✳ Sit with your legs stretched out in front of you and your feet together.
Put the baby on her back on both your legs with her head downward and resting against your feet.
Hold the baby at the ankles. Maintain this position for a minute or so before returning the baby back to the sitting position. Repeat a few times.

✳ ✳ ✳ ✳ ✳ ✳ ✳

Chapter 12

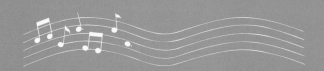

Magical Music

The Magical Music

Music has been used by mankind for centuries for the manifestation of happiness, joy and friendship.

Recent research has broadened our horizons about the benefits of listening to music. Current knowledge tells us how important music is for success in our daily lives.

The sound of music conveys feelings of love, closeness and happiness. It serves as a blanket of security for the baby. Music bonds families, integrating their minds, bodies and souls.

The first sense organ to develop in the fetus is the ear. The auditory nerve, which transmits the information of the sound from the ear to the brain, is the first sensory nerve of the body to start functioning.

The auditory system is mature enough by the 5th month of conception to be able to fully process sound.

The early and rapid maturity of the auditory system is illustrated by the fact that babies inside the womb can recognize rhythm and the pitch quite early. The first rhythm that the baby is exposed to is the heartbeat of the mother.

The maternal heart beat is a constant companion of the baby, and therefore it is no wonder that rhythm is the first musical quality the baby recognizes and appreciates while developing inside the mother's womb.

At around five months of gestational age, there is a sound explosion in the womb of the mother, which merely means that the baby's auditory sense is now wide open to receive any and every sound.

It is at about this time that the baby inside the womb is getting more accomplished in differentiating pitch of the sounds, the music and the voices the baby hears.

This is an extremely important step because being able to differentiate pitch is the first step in acquiring language capabilities. This eventually leads to good reading skills and good communication.

It is therefore highly recommended that the mother starts rich and good quality verbal communication with the baby inside the womb at around five months of gestation.

Babies not only hear but also remember the sounds to which they were exposed to, while inside the womb. This is why newborns demonstrate through their behavior that they can perceive the difference between their mother tongue and other languages. The fact that they can remember has been demonstrated in many studies.

Studies have shown that babies recognize and prefer music that their mothers listened to while they were still in the womb.

The centers for music and language are entirely separate, but they lie very close to each other in the brain. They develop roughly in the same pattern and at the same time.

It has been proven beyond doubt that exposure to classical music, especially Mozart, plays an important role in developing the mental faculties of an infant.

Exposing the developing baby to an abundance of verbal language can stimulate the ability to create and perform music.

Music therapy today is used for healing, relaxation and motivation, among others. It also serves as a tool for enhancing mental capabilities and learning faculties.

Music plays an important role in the lives of fetuses, infants and children. Scientific evidence proves that the immense power of music is an ideal tool for helping our children grow to be brighter & more intelligent.

Effects of the magic of music

O   Music helps to establish communication between the baby in the womb and the outside world.

O   It helps in the stimulation and the growth of the brain and the neural connections in the brain. In short, it serves as the right tonic for maturing brain.

> Exposure to music helps increase creativity and results in higher IQ levels in later life.

O Music has a calming effect on the developing mind and the brain of the fetus in the womb. It can help in shaping the emotional components of the infant's personality.

O Music enhances the motor development of babies with the result that they sit, crawl, stand and walk earlier.

O When premature and sick babies being treated in intensive care units, are exposed to music, they tend to put on weight faster, recover more rapidly, fight infections better, have a better chance of survival and also leave the hospital early.

O Music improves language skills. Therefore, babies are able to learn to read and write early.

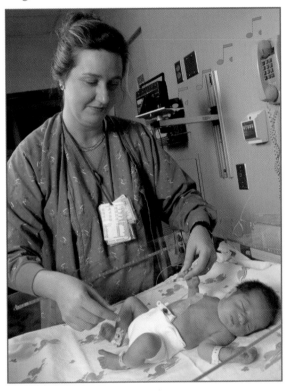

O Babies exposed to music are good with numbers, calculations and have good mathematical skills.

O Music develops and enhances memorization skills.

○ Babies exposed to music from the time they are in the mother's womb are generally born as happy, healthy and relaxed babies.

○ Music helps to enhance creative skills.

○ It improves self confidence and makes individuals more communicative, expressive and socially likeable.

○ Children exposed to music are better learners and tend to have a higher IQ later on, compared with other children of the same age group who have not been exposed to much music.

Chapter 13

SIGN LANGUAGE

SIGN LANGUAGE

We all know very well that not being able to express ourselves verbally and be understood can be very frustrating. This very commonly results in agitation and temper tantrums, which we often see in small babies.

Thus, sign language becomes an important tool to help in establishing communication between the baby and caregivers, a long time before actual verbal communication can take place.

Starting to communicate with your baby through sign language will satisfy your baby's emotional needs and will result in a happy baby and a satisfied caregiver.

What is Sign Language?

It is a means of using our hands and gestures to convey our thoughts and our needs to another person.

All babies will use sign language in one form or another before they are able to speak. Stop and think! We use sign language often in our daily lives when we talk to our little ones, without even realizing it.

Why do we do that? Well, we do it with the purpose of making it simpler and easier for the baby to understand what we are trying to convey to her. We are also, in turn, looking for gestures from the baby to understand what the baby is trying to say to us.

This exercise continues until the baby starts communicating verbally. Do you remember how often you have used your index finger to teach the meaning of the word "no" to your baby?

How many times have you put your index finger on your lips to say "quiet?" How many times have you waved your hand to teach the baby "bye?" We create and use the signs all along, especially to instill discipline and good manners in our little ones.

Have we ever paused to think that in the same context the baby also might want or need to use signs to express her wants and desires? What makes us sure that the baby feels happy and satisfied in waving "bye" by moving her hands?

Maybe she would want to carry this experience forward by learning to express the desire to get a bottle of milk when hungry or to be able to express the desire to be changed when soiled.

We have often seen that babies undergo a period of temper tantrums toward the latter part of their second year of life. This is because their needs and wants have suddenly increased. However, the ability to communicate verbally has not yet matched this desire, and this frustration leads to temper tantrums. Fortunately, this is only a temporary phase. It will last for a few months till the time they are able to express themselves in words.

We already know that "**all babies are born super intelligent.**"
They perceive and understand things a lot better than we think they do.

Taking an overall average, babies will start to pronounce words by 16 months of age and will speak a short sentence of two or three words by about 18 to 20 months.

Around the age of three months, all vital senses such as, vision, hearing and sense of touch are beginning to develop at a great speed.

At about five months, babies undergo a period of rapid muscular growth and coordination.

Between seven and eight months, they become great explorers of their surroundings. Their physical and mental activity increases tremendously. They want to explore every nook and corner, reach out and grab everything in sight, and will want to get into the details of everything they can lay their hands on.

Sign Language

While all this development is taking place, they want to express a lot of it in words -- if they could only talk.

Since they are deprived of this virtue at this stage of life, they express themselves through temper tantrums and crying.

Experiments have proved that if they could convey what they wanted to say, by using their hand movements and gestures, the result would be a much happier and more intelligent baby.

This is where **sign language** comes in.

Sign language is not about creating an alien language, but simply a matter of using purposeful hand movements and body language to convey and receive messages. The use of sign language can be started as soon as babies start to develop a reasonable control of their muscle movements and coordination of the hands.

A good time to start using sign language with your infant is around six months of age.

Will signing hamper the development of normal language?

We know that babies are born pre-programmed for the acquisition of language, and we also know that speech and language develop in a universal pattern in babies of all races and regions.

Babies will produce cooing sounds at two months of age, will babble at about six months and will start to put all their vocal skills together to produce purposeful sounds toward the end of the first year.

They may even be able to produce their first word at this time. No matter what amount of sign language you use with your baby, these milestones for the development of speech and language remain unchanged. Therefore, using sign language will not hinder the progress and development of normal language. On the contrary, it makes the subsequent development of the language much easier. Being able to communicate through sign language keeps the babies much more relaxed because their needs are expressed and taken care of. This in turn leads to an emotionally sound and intelligent baby. Studies conducted by Dr. Linda Acredolo and Dr. Susan Goodwyn at the University of California have shown that babies exposed to symbolic gestures learned to speak much earlier than babies not exposed to signing. Their research also supported the fact that the signing babies scored higher in intelligence and vocabulary tests. They have even published an excellent book "Baby Signs" which is worthwhile reading for every parent.

How much Sign Language do we use?

There is no hard-and-fast rule about the amount of sign language to be taught to a baby.

In my practice, I advise parents to use enough signs that to let the babies communicate easily and to help them in their daily physical and social needs.

The need will vary from one baby to another and will also depend on the choice of signs you would like to stress.

The signs that are recommended in our program are based on the American Sign Language (ASL) system. These are the ones most widely used and are standardized.

Parents have been known to develop their **own signs**, ones that are convenient to them.

I encourage you to use any signs that help the baby to communicate with you and vice versa.

Any custom-made sign is good enough as long as you are consistent and it serves the purpose. In any case, this is a temporary phase and will last only till the baby acquires spoken language.

PREREQUISITES FOR SIGNING

❖ Communicate and sign, looking directly toward the baby's face and pronounce the words along with the signs.

❖ Do not try to sign to the baby when she is tired, sleepy or irritable. It may be of no use and end up in more frustration for both of you.

❖ Sign with the baby at the right time, and correlate it with the appropriate activity. For example, sign for milk just prior to giving a bottle to the baby.
Likewise teach the sign for flower while in the park or the garden, and show the flower to the baby.

❖ It is important to use the correct signs and be consistent with the signs. If you use a different sign for the same word on different occasions, the baby is bound to get confused.

❖ Repetition and reinforcement are extremely important. The more you use a particular sign, the easier it becomes for the baby to learn it.

❖ Once the baby has learned to recognize the sign, encourage the baby to participate by repeating the sign back to you.

❖ Use plenty of vocal language and facial expressions when using the sign language with your baby. It helps in reinforcing the sign in the baby's mind.

❖ Do not look for immediate results, otherwise both you and the baby will get frustrated. It will take some time for the baby to learn what is going on. Once the baby has learned a few signs, it gets easier for her to learn more.

❖ Be patient with the baby and make the Sign Language Program a happy game for the baby.

It is recommended to start signing with the baby from the age of six months. The baby may not respond immediately, but the information fed now will be retrieved with positive results later.

The most commonly used and recommended signs are:-

Milk 	**Eat** 
☞ Milk - Open and close the hand a few times as if milking a cow.	☞ Eat - Point the fingers and thumb toward the mouth.
Drink 	**More** 
☞ Drink - As if holding a glass, place the thumb at the lower lip. Tilt the head backward to signify drinking action.	☞ More - The fingers and the thumb of both hands are held together and tapped at the tips a few times.

Change

↳ Change - Place one fist against the other at chest level and move at the knuckles in opposite directions.

Water

↳ Water - The thumb and the little finger are held together with the other fingers stretched out. Tap the angle of the mouth with the index finger.

Banana

↳ Banana - Place curved index finger of one hand along the straight index finger of the other hand and move up and down.

Apple

↳ Apple - Place the curved index finger on the cheek and twist a few times.

Baby

 Baby ~ Place the forearms one on top of the other and rock from side to side.

Flower

 Flower ~ Holding the fingers and the thumb of the hand together, touch one side of the nose and then the other.

Cat

 Cat ~ The index finger and the thumb are held together at the corner of the mouth with the other fingers fanning out.

Dog

 Dog ~ The tip of the middle finger and the thumb are held together and snapped a few times.

Up

Down

☝ Up - Point the index finger upward.

☝ Down - Point the index finger downward.

Book

No

☝ Book - With both hands together open and close your palms.

☝ No - The first two fingers of the hand are held together and opened and closed a few times against the extended thumb.

Stop

Car

Stop - Hold out an open hand flat with the other hand coming down on it sideways.

Car - Hold both fists at chest level and move in opposite directions as if turning a steering wheel.

Chapter 14

The Intelligent Brain

The Intelligent Brain

Our brain is the center of our intelligence. This three-pound mass that sits in our skulls is the biggest wonder of this world. It is the window through which we discover and see the other wonders on the Earth and beyond.

There are billions of people on the surface of this earth, but not a single brain is identical to another in terms of its character and the way it functions.

It is the amazing thought process of our brains that can take us from Niagara Falls to the Great Wall of China, to the wandering wild animals of Africa, and to the peak of Himalayas within just a few seconds.

Each one of us is so proud of our brain and its capabilities that calling someone brainless is probably the worst form of insult for a human being.

The brain of the fetus grows most rapidly between 10 to 26 weeks of conception, and at that time, as many as 250,000 brain cells are produced every minute.

The newborn's brain contains 100 billion nerve cells called neurons.

All of these cells make numerous connections with each other over the first three years of life.

This gives us the magnitude and the complexity of trillions of connections between these cells.

Through these interconnections, the neurons transmit information from one to another. This ability to communicate and send information between the neurons differentiates them from the other cells in the body.

By six months of age, the infant's brain is 50 percent of the adult brain weight, 70 percent by the end of the first year and 90 percent of the adult brain weight by three years of age.

Six Months

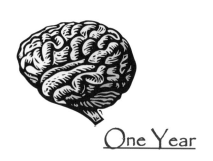

One Year

Three Years

The majority of brain growth therefore occurs in the first year of life, which is the reason the first year is a very crucial time in the life of an infant.

Because the brain is growing so rapidly in the first year, and the neurons are forming connections between one another at an incredible rate, it is critically important to expose the infant to intelligent, intense and high quality stimulation.

Why are neuron connections so important?

⇩

Each time your baby turns around to look at a red balloon floating over his cot, a spark ignites between the eye and the brain and a connection is formed.

When you hold the little bell that you got for the baby and shake it close to his ear, the tinkle sends a wave from the ear to the brain and forms a connection.

Similarly with each sense that the baby uses alone or in combination with another sense, connections keep forming .

These connections form at a startling rate in the first three years of life.

It is these connections of the nerve cells that enable the vital senses of our body to communicate with each other and function as a unit. Without the integration of our vital senses, such as vision, hearing, speech, touch, smell and taste, life would be impossible.

Connections between the neurons cease to form after the first three years. Intelligent parenting in the first three years of life, and particularly in the first year, is therefore of vital importance.

The brain cell (neuron) consists of three parts

The cell body

The axon

The dendrites

The axon, coming out from the cell body, sends information to the other cells in the form of small electrical impulses.

In the same way, dendrites carry information coming into the cell body of the neuron.

The axon of one neuron will communicate with the dendrite of the other neuron for receiving and relaying messages.

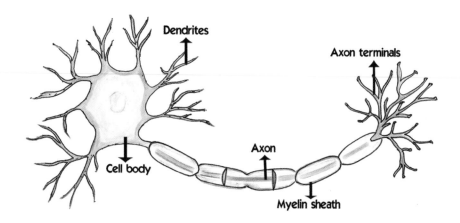

172

The point at which the axon and the dendrite meet is called a synapse.

Since there are trillions of these connections, sending electrical impulses from one to another, it is like a complicated electrical network.

Supposing this electrical network were made up of live wires without insulation. The result would be enormous number of short-circuits resulting in the breakdown of this electrical network.

In order to safeguard against this catastrophe, the axons are covered by an insulating material called myelin which is a fatty substance.

In simpler terms, myelination is like a process of coating electrical wires with rubber insulation.

This not only provides safety against short-circuit but also helps the speed that impulses are relayed at.

Without myelination, this complex network cannot function, and nervous tissue will not be able to send messages between the billions of cells that work as a unit in this system.

The process of myelination begins in early pregnancy and continues throughout childhood.

The process of myelination is at its peak during the rapid growth of the brain in the first year of life, and myelination of the major nerves in the body is virtually completed by four years of age.

Myelination proceeds from the head toward the toes and from the center of the body toward the periphery (i.e. toward the fingers and the toes).

It is critically important, especially in the first year of life, to provide the infant with intelligent and high-quality stimulation of all the important senses such as vision, hearing, feel and touch.

The fact that neural connections will cease to form after three years makes the first three years most critical for changing the entire future life of an individual.

Experiences of infancy and early childhood are critical and will determine how we behave in later life.

It is said that the level of intelligence of a child is directly related to the level of intelligence of the care givers.

Poor stimulation in the early years of life can lead to irreversible damage to intelligence. The importance of early stimulation can be rightly summed up in one sentence: " Catch them early and catch them fresh."

A human brain is like a pre-programmed video camera which has automatically been switched on prior to birth. Ironically, it does not have a switch off mechanism.

It records all that it sees, hears and experiences. It is therefore important to have the brain capture and record good quality experiences.

This computer of the brain is far more superior to any computer on Earth. It can integrate all that has been fed into it, and has the ability to conform the data of experiences and knowledge in a way that no other computer can.

The early experiences of childhood have an everlasting impression on the way we think, feel and perceive the world around us.

The classical example of how surroundings affect the growing brain and other vital senses has been well documented in many tales of child abuse. In all these cases, infants and children were deprived of proper environment and stimulation in the first few years of life. The lesson learnt from these sad incidents is common.

Proper and intelligent stimulation of the human brain and vital senses should be carried out from the beginning. Deprivation of proper stimulation will always lead to irreversible damage to intelligence and in most cases to physical development as well.

The Intelligent Brain

An infant's brain is like soft clay. It can be moulded and reshaped in any way we want.

As time goes by, this plasticity will go away and at some point it becomes virtually impossible to make any headway with the hardened brain, no matter how much stimulation is provided.

The capabilities of the human mind are limitless. Even the best of scientists cannot give the exact configuration of the memory, speed or functions of this computer. It indeed is an amazing and precious vital organ.

I again stress, do not under estimate the capabilities of your baby's brain. Stimulate it to its maximum and you will achieve tremendous results. Never forget :
>   All babies are born with Super Intelligence.

Each piece of information that we give to the infant is called a unit of knowledge. Each unit of knowledge is like a building block. The more blocks we use, the higher the building is going to be.

Building knowledge has no limitations. The higher and stronger it is, the more intelligent is the individual.

The ability to excel in life and achieve greater heights is directly related to the level of one's intelligence.

The central nervous system is divided into three major sections.

~ The cerebral cortex ~

~ The brain stem ~

~ The spinal cord ~

The cerebral cortex is divided into two hemispheres, the right and the left, which are lodged in the skull.

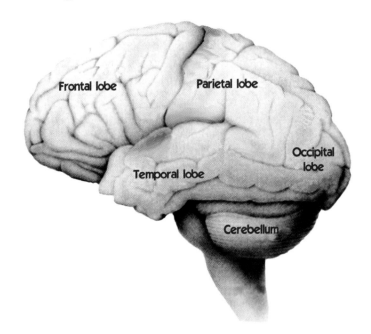

Each of these hemispheres is further divided into four sections or lobes which are separated from one another by deep grooves.

The frontal lobe, which lies toward the front of the skull, is responsible for motor control and coordination of the functions of other cortical areas of the brain.

177

The temporal lobe, which lies around the temple of the skull, is responsible for hearing and speech.

The parietal lobe lies toward the top and back of the skull and is responsible for spatial perception.

The occipital lobe, lying right at the back of the skull, is responsible for vision.

At the back of the skull adjacent to the brain stem, is the part of the brain called the cerebellum. The main function of the cerebellum is to maintain balance and motor coordination. No wonder the cerebellum grows fastest during the first year of life. This is a busy time for the infant's motor development and motor coordination.

At the base of the cerebral cortex is the brain stem. The brain stem controls actions such as sucking, blinking, sleeping and even breathing.

The brain stem at birth is one of the most highly developed areas of the central nervous system.

From the base of the brain stem down to our spine extends the spinal cord.

Nerves emerge from the spinal cord and branch out to specific areas such as muscles, skin, bone and joints.

These spinal nerves form the communication network between these tissues and the brain. They relay messages to the brain and carry orders from the brain back to these tissues.

This is how we respond reflexively, withdrawing our hand if it comes in contact with a sharp or a hot object.

Now that we know the capabilities of this magnificent organ, let us not leave any facet untouched or any leaf unturned.

Critical Windows of Opportunities

Critical Windows exist for all the important senses and they are periods during which learning takes place at a very fast speed and with effortless ease. During this time whatever information is laid down in the brain will never be forgotten.

Critical Windows of Opportunities for all vital senses such as vision, hearing, language and speech have certain important time frames when they will open one by one. This happens in the first few months and years of life. These windows of opportunities will then close one by one in a particular order. The windows of opportunities have to be recognized and appreciated because once closed shut they will not open again.

Between the ages of four to eight months there is a growth spurt and an explosion in the faculty of the vision of the baby. This is the Critical Window of Opportunity for the sense of Vision.

Critical Window of Opportunity for the sense of Hearing

Between four to eight months of age, auditory cells are developing at a rapid speed, and this is a period of high receptivity for sounds.

This period of enhanced receptivity will last till about ten months of age. This is therefore the critical window for auditory stimulation and one should make good use of this time by playing music, talking to the baby and engaging in other means of auditory stimulation.

Critical Window for the development of Language.

The critical period for hearing also coincides with the Critical Window for the development of Language. This critical window for the acquisition of language is very important for the development of vocabulary and eventual language skills. This is the period when the child registers the phonemes in his brain.

Critical Window for Motor Development

For the first three to four months the newborn is totally dependent on the caregiver as he is unable to move around on his own.

By the fifth or sixth month the child starts to make purposeful movements. Motor coordination and muscle strength gets better. This period signifies the beginning of the Critical Window for Motor Development.

A major change takes place in the life of the little one at this time. He will soon become a great explorer of the world around him. It is very important to provide the child with as much Motor Stimulation as possible during this time.

It is important to understand the need for the the Stimulation of all the vital senses at the right time, and take full advantage of all the Critical Windows of Opportunities.

Intelligent stimulation in the first few years can lead to a substantial increase in IQ as early as five years of age. Such children will always do well later in life due to the early head start.

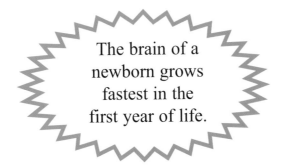

The brain of a newborn grows fastest in the first year of life.

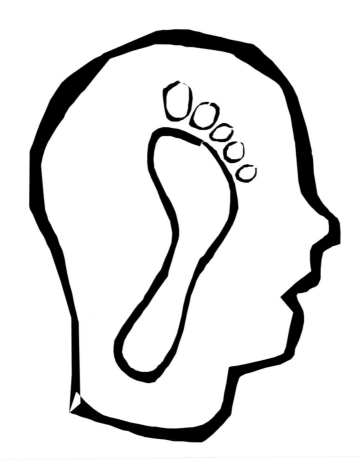

Chapter 15

The Amazing
RIGHT BRAIN

The Amazing RIGHT BRAIN

The human brain is divided into two halves, the right and the left.

The cerebral cortex of the right hemisphere is responsible for the development of artistic faculties such as music, emotion, sounds and intuitive thinking.

The cortex of the left hemisphere is mainly responsible for reasoning, logic and cognitive or analytic skills such as language and math.

The left brain works like a slow computer, operating consciously and methodically. This is the linguistic and the logical brain. The right brain works at high speed with an automatic processing function. It is the imaging and the artistic brain.

If proper stimulation is provided to both hemispheres at the same time, it will promote intelligence and increase the IQ of the growing child.

The Amazing Right Brain

After a baby is born, the right brain is functionally more active than the left brain.

The period of enhanced activity of the right brain lasts from birth until age three.

Thereafter is a period of transition, between ages three to six, when the left brain gradually gains more dominance over the right brain.
By six years of age, the left brain becomes completely dominant over the right brain.

It is therefore extremely important to take advantage of this critical period and provide maximum stimulation to the right brain and its faculties from birth until age six.

After six, it becomes difficult to explore the amazing potential of the right brain.

Recently, educators have started emphasizing the development of the right brain and its capabilities.

The left brain processes information via language, while the right brain processes information through images.

The right brain works on the basis of capturing images, and images form the units of information for the right brain.

The left brain's memory is therefore linguistic, whereas the right brain's memory is imagery or photographic.

Although the two sides of the brain have distinct functions, they of course function as a single unit, hand-in-hand with each other.

The left brain perceives information slowly and connects each unit of information in a linear fashion. This is called the Propositional Method of memorization. The right brain's system is called the Appositional Method. The right brain achieves this through its capabilities for photographic memory.

Because of this, the right brain can memorize and store massive quantities of information very rapidly.

The Amazing Right Brain

In 1981, Professor Roger Sperry of California Institute of Technology received the Noble Prize for medicine for his research on the functioning and the capabilities of the right brain.

The special functions of the right brain are:

Image visualization

High-speed mass memorization (Photographic Memory)

High-speed processing of information

These functions of the right brain form the basis of The Infant Stimuli Program.

Image visualization is the ability to perceive an image in the subconscious mind. We can train the brain to perceive images of events and incidents. Using this imaging technique we can enhance our physical and mental potential in our daily lives.

Top athletes such as gymnasts, and golfers among others use the imaging technique to train and produce better results. Today, imaging techniques are also being used successfully in the field of medicine for treating phobias and other illnesses.

Critical ailments such as cancer have longer periods of remission when imaging techniques of the right brain are used along with regular medication and the treatment these patients receive.

Children are fortunately born with imaging ability, but this ability diminishes with age. If infants are trained to develop this ability early, they can achieve incredible results for the rest of their lives.

All children are born with excellent memory skills.

The capability of the right brain for high-speed mass memory enables it to memorize massive information at a very rapid speed. The right brain not only memorizes large volumes of information quickly, but also has this magical ability to process this volume of information and store it faster than any computer.

This is the unique capability, that has been used by geniuses such as Mozart and Schubert in creating and playing masterpieces without referring to music notes.

Stimulation of the right brain can be started from early infancy with great success by using the Flash Card training technique.

The key to the Flash Card training method is to present a large volume of information very rapidly.

FLASH CARDS

Flash Cards are rectangular white cards with a piece of information printed on them. Each Flash card message is a unit of knowledge. There are nine different categories of Flash cards that are used in this stimulation program. The sizes and the number of cards in each category are as follows:

Categories	Number of Cards	Size
Animals	24	8x6 inches
Fruits and Vegetables	24	8x6 inches
Common objects	24	8x6 inches
Colors	12	8x6 inches
Shapes	12	8x6 inches
Numbers	10	8x6 inches
Alphabets	26	8x6 inches
Words	24	9x4 inches
Dots	50	9x8 inches

The first-year program has been divided into four quarters of three months. The usage and schedule table of the Flash cards has been incorporated in the individual quarterly programs.

Flash Cards should be presented to the child at distance of 18 to 20 inches from her eyes. Each Flash Card has the subject printed on the back of the card so it is easy for you to tell the child aloud about the information without looking at the card. Cards must be shown rapidly at a rate of one card every second to derive optimal benefit from the program.

Stimulation through the use of the dot cards helps babies to learn how to count and enhances the calculating abilities of the right brain.

ৡঌ

The idea of presenting the information of the Flash Cards is not for memorization, but to develop the imaging ability and the photographic memory of the right brain.

ples of the flash cards used in this program are presented in
ing pages. You can make your own flash cards according to
nes given earlier or order a full set of the flash cards from:

www.infantstimuli.com

Flash Cards of Fruits and Vegetables

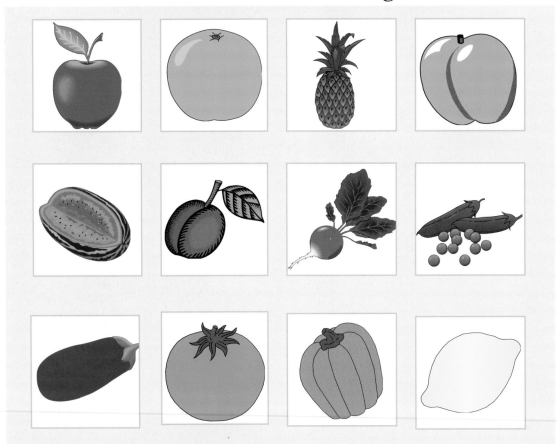

Flash Cards of Alphabets

A to Z

Flash Cards of Dots 1 to 50

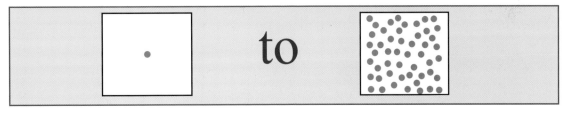

Flash Cards of Animals

Flash Cards of Numbers

Flash Cards of Objects

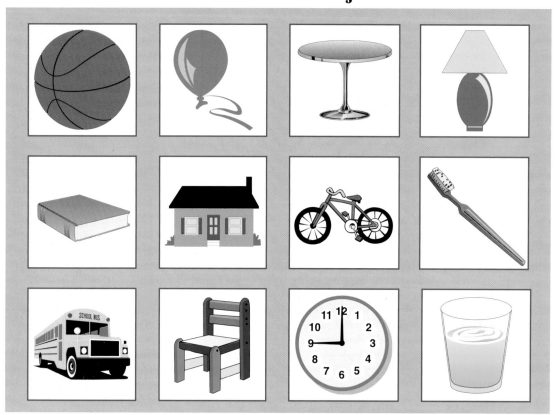

Flash Cards of Patterns

Flash Cards of Shapes

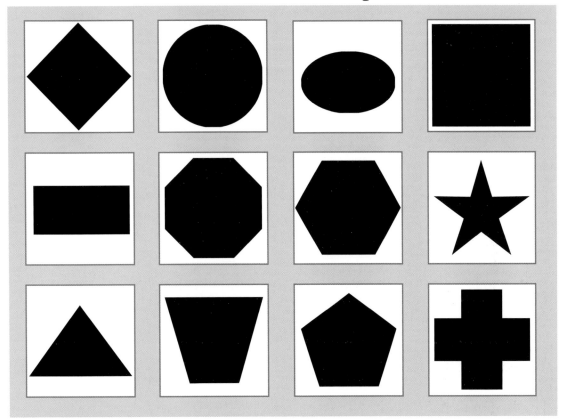

Flash Cards of Patterns

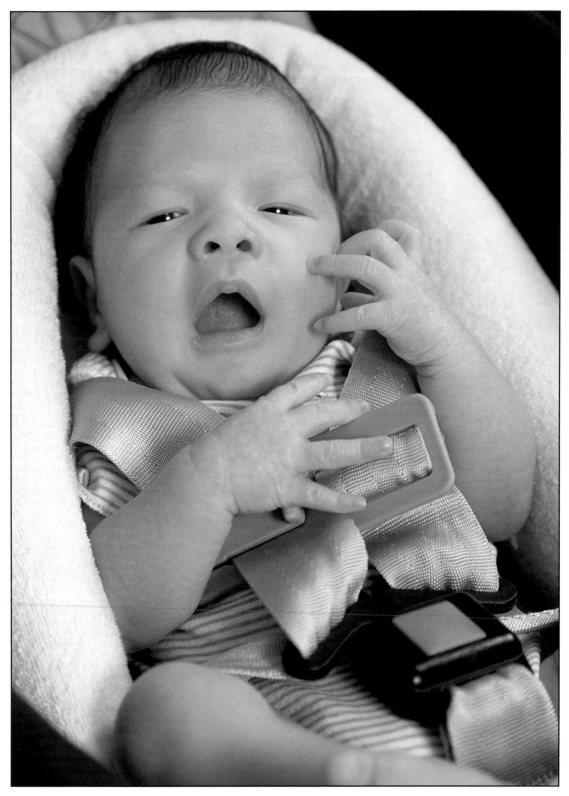

Chapter 16

MILESTONES IN THE FIRST YEAR OF LIFE

Milestones are indications for your baby's physical and mental development.

There are four important areas to be taken into consideration:

Large Motor Movements

Coordination and Fine Motor Movements

Hearing and Speech

Emotional Development and Social Behavior

A knowledge of Milestones of your baby is important for you to assess whether your baby's growth and development is within the normal parameters at a given age.

Medical or professional advice should be sought if you are in any doubt about the behavior and the progressive development of your baby.

Milestones
(First Quarter)

Large Motor Movements

Involuntary Reflexes

★ **The sucking reflex:**

At birth and in the first few weeks, the baby demonstrates an involuntary sucking reflex. The baby will suck at anything soft placed in the mouth. This reflex is also manifested many times during sleep when the baby will make involuntary sucking sounds and motions.

★ **Rooting Reflex:**

The rooting reflex is when the baby turns his face to the right if gently stroked on the right cheek and involuntarily turns to her left if stroked on the left cheek.

★ **Moro's reflex:**

When startled by a loud noise or any disturbance, the infant will throw her arms and legs in the air and arch her back. This is known as the involuntary Moro's reflex.

★ **Fetal reflex:**

In the first month, the infant will usually sleep in a fetal position, with the knees and elbows drawn in and tucked in toward the tummy.

★ **Grasp reflex:**

In the first few weeks, the baby has an involuntary grasp reflex, and will keep the fists tightly clenched. This reflex will start to disappear by the second month.

Voluntary Reflexes

❖ Head and Neck Control:

In the first four weeks, head control is poor and the head is wobbly at the neck. Head and neck control starts to get better in the second month. If placed on the tummy, the baby will try to raise the head and shoulder in the midline for a few seconds. In the third month, head and neck control is definitely a lot better, and when placed on the tummy, the baby will raise the head and upper body by pushing up at the forearms. By now, the head is steady and the baby will move the head and neck from side to side.

❖ Arms and Legs Control:

In the second month, the baby starts to get some control over the movements of the arms and legs. By the third month, the movements of the arms and legs are much more powerful. The baby will kick vigorously using both legs.

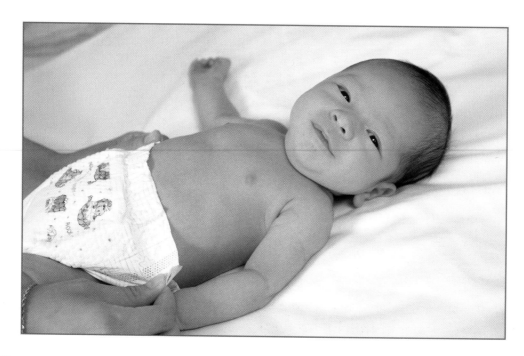

❖ Hand Control:

Your baby will bring both hands together from the sides to the midline over the chest by the third month, and will clasp both hands in front of her.

❖ Back Control:

In the third month when held at the wrists, your baby will pull to sit with no head lag. When held in the sitting position, the back will be fairly straight with only a little lag of the lower back.

❖ Foot Control:

In the third month, the baby enjoys being held standing firm on her feet. She holds her back straight with good head and neck control.

Coordination & Fine Motor Movements

✳ First Month:

In the first month the vision of your baby is limited to 13 inches from the face, and the baby prefers to look at only black and white objects.

When presented with a black and white object within the visual field in the midline of the face, the baby will follow the object slowly, six inches to the left and right, and six inches up and down.

In the first month, the grasp reflex is quite strong, and the infant will hold on to a rattle tightly.

> Sense of touch is the baby's most advanced faculty at birth

✳ Second Month:

In the second month, the baby will try to reach for an object within the visual range but not very accurately.

The grasp reflex in the second month starts to fade away; the hands are held more open and now the fingers are more flexible.

The baby can now hold on to a small object placed in the hand and move it around and toward the

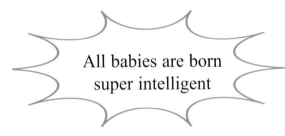

All babies are born
super intelligent

✱ Third Month:

At this stage, the visual field is getting better, and the baby will watch objects and people with interest.

The baby can now follow a dangling object 6 to 12inches from her face. She now has the visual ability to follow objects from left to right in a half circle and up toward the top of the head and down toward the chin.

At three months, babies like to watch the movements of their own hands. They engage in finger play by clasping and unclasping the hands, or pressing the palms of the hands against one another.

The baby will hold a rattle now for a few minutes and move the rattle toward the face, invariably hitting herself on the face.

At three months while sitting in your lap, the baby looks at story books with interest and will reach out to touch pictures.

Hearing & Speech

- Just a few days after birth, the baby is capable of recognizing your voice, and enjoys listening to human voices.

- The baby will react to sudden sounds with a startle, and will make eye contact when held close and talked to.

- By the second month, you will be able to determine why the baby is crying by the tone of the cry. You can differentiate the cry of hunger from that of the cry of boredom or cry for attention. The baby will stop crying when picked up and spoken to.

Sense of hearing in the fetus is well developed by the 24th week of pregnancy

- The baby will start making cooing sounds in the second month, and will vocalize delightfully when spoken to.

- In the third month, the baby will instinctively stop and listen to the soft sound of a bell or a rattle and may turn the head slowly toward the source of sound.

- By this stage, the baby recognizes quite a few sounds, such as the sound of running water at bath time and the sounds of food being prepared. The baby shows excitement at hearing human voices.

Emotional Development & Social Behavior

> A newborn baby enjoys human company and responding to voices. As early as just a few days after birth, babies can recognize the voice and the body smell of their parents.

> All babies enjoy being cuddled and held close.

Babies can see, hear, taste, and feel touch even before birth

> By six weeks of age, the baby will give the first meaningful smile when spoken to.

> Even as early as in the first month, the baby starts responding positively when being spoken to, and by the second month onward, shows enjoyment and excitement over the care given by parents or care givers.

> Your baby will start to recognize familiar music by the third month and will show excitement when the same music is played.

> In the third month, the baby starts to imitate adults, sticking out her tongue or opening and closing her mouth.

Poor stimulation in early years can lead to irreversible damage to intelligence

Newborns recognize their mothers' faces as early as two days after birth

> By the third month the baby is much more settled. She will be more interactive, responding with bigger, brighter smiles, and certainly crying less unless really annoyed.

> Now the baby enjoys human company more than in the earlier months and looks forward to interaction with parents, care-givers and siblings. The baby fixes eyes purposefully on the mother's face while feeding, and is always looking for communication.

Milestones
(Second Quarter)

Large Motor Movements

☙❧

☒ By the fourth month, the involuntary grasp reflex has disappeared and grasping has now become a deliberate and voluntary movement.

☒ Your baby can now sit upright with support, has established good head control and can turn the head in all directions with ease.

☒ The baby can now turn over from left to right and right to left, but still cannot roll over on his own.

☙❧

Connections between nerve cells will cease to form after the first three years

☙❧

☒ In the fifth month, your baby will be able to roll over comfortably from back to front and vice versa.
He will also start to move around the floor by rolling and turning.

☒ When lying on his back, he will push firmly against the sides of the cot, using the soles of the feet.

☙❧

Massaging and stroking the infant develops bonding and increases emotional and physical attachment between the mother and the baby.

☒ When you grasp his hands in a lying down position, he will readily pull himself up to a sitting or a standing position.

☒ At six months, the baby can roll over easily and enjoy twisting and turning in all directions.

☒ In the sixth month when lying on his back, the baby will raise his head and look at his feet. At this time, he will also lift his legs and start reaching out to grab his toes.

☒ Your baby can now sit very well with a straight back and perfect head control with minimal support, and also for some time without support.

☒ When placed face down on the floor, the baby can raise his head, neck, shoulders and chest by supporting himself on the palms of his hands with the arms extended. He looks in all directions now and is also making attempts to propel himself forward.

Coordination & Fine Motor Movements

Connections are strengthened by repeated and good stimulation

⌘

At the age of four months, your baby's eyesight is well developed. He can see all colors, focuses well and can see right across the room, just like an adult.

He will try and reach out to grab objects placed close to him, and after grabbing waves the toy in the air.

By the fifth month, he will watch and follow your movements around the room with interest.

The baby can now reach out for toys with more accuracy and will hold the toy with a very firm grasp. He shows a lot of interest in toys such as rattles and bells, and gets excited at the noise they produce.

⌘

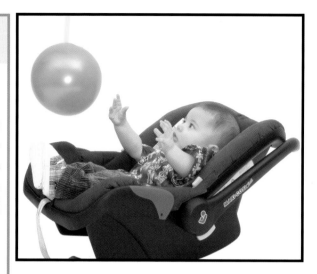

☒ At six months, your baby can use his whole hand to grasp objects, and can pass a toy from one hand to another in a synchronized movement.

☒ If a toy falls from the hand within the visual field, the baby will follow the moving toy to its resting place.

Pre-birth bonding with the baby is as essential as bonding after birth

☒ If the fallen toy is outside the visual field, the baby will generally forget about it or search briefly in the immediate vicinity.

☒ At this stage, the baby will enjoy dropping toys deliberately, and will reach out to pick them up repeatedly.

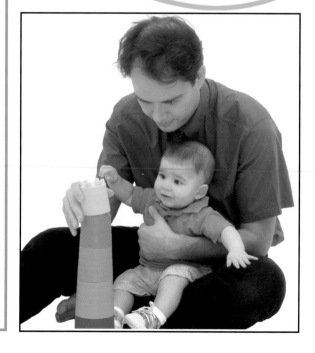

☒ At feeding time, the baby will try to grab the spoon or the feeding bottle.

Hearing & Speech

At four months of age, your baby is becoming very social. He will listen with interest to different sounds and move his head in that particular direction.

At this age, the baby loves human voices, especially the mother's, and may vocalize to draw your attention.

The baby is starting to look curiously at his surroundings. He gets excited when looking at himself in the mirror and tries to reach out for his reflection.

Around the fifth month, the baby will pick up objects within the visual field and look at them meaningfully, with a lot of interest.

At five months the baby will also start babbling aloud and vocalize excitedly when spoken to. He will turn to the source of the sound, trying to locate it.

At six months, your baby will convey to you his moods, will laugh when happy and excited and cries and screams when angry.

At this stage, your baby will start responding a lot more. He will gurgle, laugh, scream and squeal aloud and repeatedly while playing. Common sounds are goo, adah, der, aroo, etc.

Enhancing language skills increases IQ levels

Emotional Development & Social Behavior

★ At four months of age, your baby is more playful. He will scream, chuckle and squeal when he is in a happy mood and will also begin to use facial expressions to go with these situations.

★ He is now more aware of his surroundings and enjoys the regular routines such as changing and feeding. He gets excited at bath time at the sound of running water, and enjoys splashing around.

★ By the fifth month, the baby will develop a sleep pattern and is attentive and active when awake. He enjoys playing by himself, as he is curious and is also discovering something new all the time.

★ At six months, your baby is quite friendly with your friends and relatives, but tends to be shy occasionally with strangers. He shows excitement when in the company of small children, smiles, vocalizes and shouts to draw attention, and wants to join them in play. He enjoys being cuddled, tickled and moved around. At six months the baby will also start responding to his name.

Milestones
Third Quarter

Large Motor Movements

- Your seven-month-old baby can now raise her shoulders, chest and tummy very easily off the floor by bearing weight on her outstretched hands.

- She can propel forward with her chest and tummy raised off the floor.

- She can now roll over easily from back to front and vice versa.

- She pulls her feet toward her face and puts her toes in her mouth.

- At seven months when you hold her in a standing position, supporting under the arms, she will bear the weight very easily with a firm straight back.

Milestones in the Seventh, Eighth and Ninth Month

- At eight months, she will be able to crawl both forward and backward.

- When placed in a standing position, she will try to hold on and balance herself.

- When sitting close to a piece of furniture, she will try to stand, though not succeeding very well at this stage.

- At nine months of age, your baby will be sitting up unsupported.

- She can now turn around easily while crawling on the floor.

- When you make her stand, she will try to step forward on alternate feet as if attempting to walk.

- She can lean forward easily without losing her balance when attempting to reach out for a toy.

- At nine months, she will pull herself to a standing position without support, but cannot lower herself and will usually fall back with a thump.

Coordination & Fine Motor Movements

At seven months, your baby has a good firm grasp and does not drop an object when held in the hand. She can now manipulate objects with a lot of interest and passes them from one hand to the other.

The baby now explores her toys with more interest and observes the details.

At this age, the baby will use both hands with good coordination and is beginning to use the thumb and the index finger for the more accurate pincer grasp.

By the age of eight months, the pincer grasp is getting even better, and the baby can pick up small objects using the thumb and the index finger. This is when she starts to enjoy eating finger foods by herself.

Milestones in the Seventh, Eighth and Ninth Month

At nine months, you will notice the baby beginning to point at objects using the index finger.

By this stage, the baby is capable of dropping a toy voluntarily and then picking it up and placing it down with precision.

At nine months, the baby has the ability to look in the correct direction and follow a fallen or a rolling toy until it comes to a halt.

Hearing & Speech

* By seven months, your baby is well aware of the tone and the emotion in your voice. She can very well understand when the tone of your voice is happy, angry or excited.

* The baby is now more responsive to your conversation and shows an understanding of what you are trying to convey.

* You will often find your baby repeating her own sounds around the age of eight months. She has also learned how to draw your attention by shouting and screaming.

* The baby will observe you closely and with a lot of interest while you are eating and imitate the actions of your mouth as you eat.

* By nine months, the baby will be loud and vocal. She will babble in loud repetitive syllables such as dada, mama, dad mam, adaba, etc.

* At nine months, the baby will start to imitate all your vocal sounds such as smacking the lip or the slurring sound you make with your tongue.

* The baby will try to pronounce her very first words, but may not be very clear at this age.

Emotional Development & Social Behavior

* By seven months, the baby begins to remember faces of people she does not see every day.

* Now, the baby has also learned to show displeasure by throwing her body backwards and by stiffening, if you stop her doing something she was enjoying.

* At eight months, the baby can vocalize and can communicate with body language if she is bored or unhappy. She is now getting good at drawing your attention whenever she wants.

* The baby now enjoys playing peek-a-boo, attempts to look for hidden objects and shows delight by screaming after locating the object.

* The baby is curious about all her new toys and enjoys playing with more than one toy at the same time. She is keen to explore and find out everything about her toys. She is also learning to be possessive about her own toys and does not like anyone playing with them.

* At this stage, the baby is shy with strangers and will hold on to you in a public place with strangers around.

* By nine months, baby has learned to mimic waving 'bye' and shaking the head to say 'no.'

* The baby enjoys being in the company of other children, but may not be too willing to play with them.

* At nine months, your baby can clearly distinguish between strangers and familiar faces. At this stage, babies need reassurance and they often hold on to you when approached by a stranger.

Milestones
Fourth Quarter

Large Motor Movements

- At 10 months, your little one is a master crawler. He can propel himself quite swiftly in all directions.

- He can sit with complete balance for long periods of time and can reach out for objects in all directions.

- He likes to stand up holding on to furniture and tries to take the first step. In this position he will reach out to grab a toy.

- At 11 months, he has learnt to lower himself from a standing position without slumping onto the floor. From this standing position he will look down at a toy on the floor and lean toward it to try to pick it up.

- The 12th month is full of excitement both for you and for him. He can now pull to a standing position and lower himself down comfortably.

- He can walk around holding on to the furniture, lifting one foot at a time with ease.

- He stands well with both hands held and may also stand without support for a short time.

- He may take the first, most important step of his life all on his own in the 12th month.

- He may crawl up a few stairs but is apprehensive about coming down when he looks back.

Coordination & Fine Motor Movements

- At 10 months, your baby may start to show hand preference. He can now grasp two little toys at the same time in one hand.

- He now likes to explore inside boxes and likes to get into cupboards and pull out drawers.

- Your baby at 10 months is beginning to show that he enjoys games using both hands, such as clapping and playing pat-a-cake.

- At 11 months, he is becoming quite an expert at using the thumb and the index finger with good coordination.

- He now enjoys playing with stacking toys and may build a little tower.

- He also enjoys nesting games, putting containers into one another.

- He removes lids of boxes to get in and explore the contents.

- He is beginning to show a lot of interest in pictures, and likes to turn pages of a book when you are reading to him.

- He points with the index finger at objects he wants, and vocalizes at the same time.

- Hand preference in the 12th month becomes more obvious.

- Outdoors, he will watch people, animals, passing cars and other vehicles with a lot of interest and excitement.

Hearing & Speech

* At around 10 months of age, your baby will turn toward you when you call out his name.

* Babies at this age show a lot of enjoyment in listening to music, and will move their bodies to the rhythm of the music.

* Your little one now jabbers loudly and continuously in conversational tone.

* He may start to say one or two words in a consistent manner, but not very clearly.

* He now pays attention, listens carefully and looks toward you when you speak to him.

* At eleven months, he may follow simple instructions such as give it to me, or put it back please.

* He may hand over objects to you on instructions such as, "give me the spoon," or "can I have the book please?"

* He recognizes common objects and will point them out if you ask him, as in show me the cat, or where is the dog?

* The magical first word that you have been dying to hear from him will usually come out in the 12th month, and it is usually dada, mama or bye bye.

* By the time he is approaching his first birthday, your little one knows and recognizes the other family members by their names.

Emotional Development & Social Behavior

* At 10 months, your baby is happy and content playing by himself.

* He now loves to play peek-a-boo and other games with your participation.

* He is very observant now and is learning new games quickly. He still feels very secure with you around and feels a little uneasy in the company of strangers.

* He loves to be cuddled, kissed and handled intimately, and will also kiss and cuddle in return.

* He gets frustrated and angry easily, and will start to scream and cry if he does not get what he wishes. His mood can easily swing from happy to foul and vice versa.

* He can put wooden cubes in and take them out of a cup if shown a few times.

* He enjoys simple puzzles and shows interest in sorting out puzzles.

* He concentrates on putting different shapes into a box through their appropriate openings.

* He listens with pleasure to sound-producing toys and tries to make them repeat the same sound by figuring out how it works.

* He will drink from a cup with little assistance and wants to hold the spoon at meal times, though he still cannot use it very well on his own.

* He is starting to put objects into the mouth less often now.

* If you hide his toy in front of his eyes, he will remember and quickly find the hidden toy.

* He feels comfortable and still likes to be within sight and sound of familiar people.

* He is now enjoying his regular routines and will help you at changing times by holding out his arms and legs.

The Stimulation Program

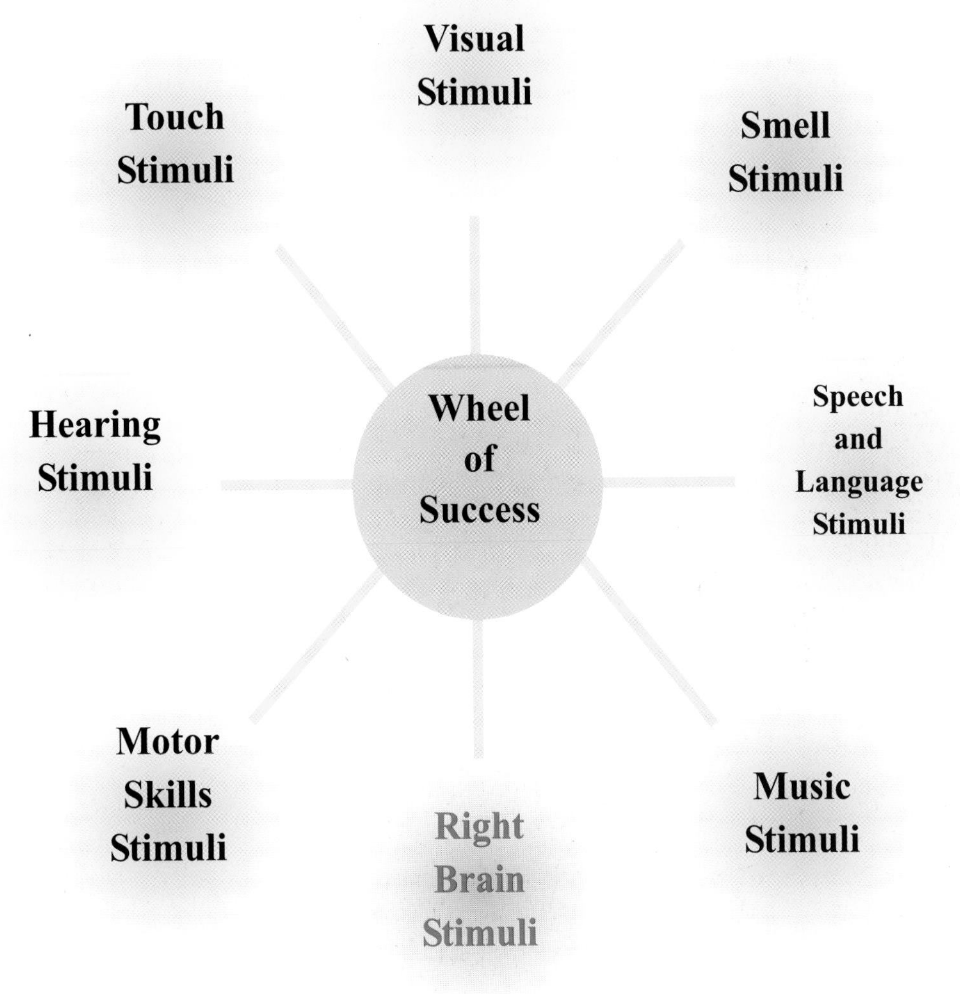

Visual
Stimuli

Touch
Stimuli

Smell
Stimuli

Hearing
Stimuli

Wheel
of
Success

Speech
and
Language
Stimuli

Motor
Skills
Stimuli

Right
Brain
Stimuli

Music
Stimuli

Stimulation Program in the

First Quarter
First, second and third Month

* To refrain from being biased toward the gender of babies 'She' and 'He' have been used in alternate chapters and quarters of the program.

* To emphasize the importance of stimulation, a few techniques have been repeated in all quarters .

Important Facts to Remember

1. The brain of the fetus grows most rapidly between 10 to 26 weeks after conception, and at that time, as many as 250,000 brain cells are forming every minute.

2. The first three years are the most crucial for development of the brain, and out of these, the first year is essentially the most important. Poor quality stimulation in early years can lead to irreversible damage to intelligence.

3. The right brain has special qualities such as, photographic memory and the ability for rapid and mass memorization. The right brain is more dominant than the left brain in the first three years of life.

4. Many recent studies have shown that the fetus starts to hear from the 24th week onward while still inside the womb. The ability to process feelings and emotion starts in the fetus during the second trimester of pregnancy.

5. A newborn has the ability to identify and recognize the mother's face as early as two days after birth. A one-week-old baby can tell the difference between the smell of her own mother's milk as compared to another woman's milk.

6. The first sense to emerge in a developing embryo is that of touch, starting from the head and proceeding to the toes. Newborns can feel soft and firm, rough and smooth, hot and cold. The sharpness of the sense of touch increases fourfold between birth and one year of age.

7. As little as an intimate first hour of close skin contact between the newborn and the mother can leave an everlasting impression on the child.

 CႽჄჄႩჄჄႩ

Questions & Answers

Before we move on to the **Stimulation Program**, it would be fair to answer some of the questions or queries arising in your mind as a parent or caregiver.

Q.1 How much time will it take me each day to follow the Stimulation Program?

Once you have read the program, you will realize that the majority of the Infant Stimulation Program revolves around the normal day-to-day activities of the baby with you. Most activities will take no more than a few minutes each, and soon the entire program will become a way of life.

Q.2 What happens if there is an interruption in the program? Do I have to start all over again?

Of course, interruptions are bound to take place. The child or you may be unwell, or just too tired on a given day. Just relax. You have not lost anything, provided the interruptions are not too frequent. Babies have a good memory and do not forget easily. You must always restart the program from where you stopped. Make this program an enjoyable experience for yourself and the baby.

Q.3 Will my child get burdened with too much information?

The brain is a vessel which never gets full nor overflows. The more you pour into it, the more it absorbs. Early stimulation aims at trying to increase the use of the brain to higher levels than the regular 4 percent. Achieving that will make the child's later learning years much easier and enjoyable. This will in turn lead to the enhancement of the child's performance in all spheres of life.

Q.4 How soon or how often can I test my baby?

The objective of stimulating the right brain is not memorization, but the stimulation of the photographic memory and mass memorization. Once the potential of the right brain has been aroused, the brain can memorize massive quantities of information in a flash. Hence the Flash Cards used in this program are an ideal tool.

Do not try to test the baby at this stage. Treat this time as data feeding time into the computer and setting up the right systems. The time for retrieval of information will come later. Once you have activated the immense capabilities of the right brain, you yourself will be amazed at the tremendous potential of your child.

The First Quarter Program

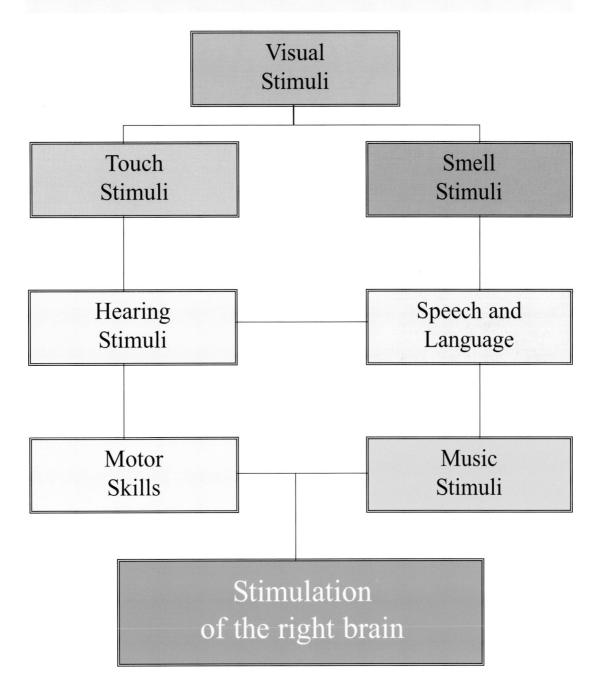

Visual Stimuli

Touch Stimuli

Smell Stimuli

Hearing Stimuli

Speech and Language

Motor Skills

Music Stimuli

Stimulation of the right brain

Vision

Stimulation in the first two months

Objectives of Visual Stimulation

Stimulate and increase concentration

Stimulate the tracking and focusing abilities of the eyes

Stimulate coordination of the eyes

Stimulate the movements of the head and neck

Stimulate eye/hand coordination

Stimulate and enrich the eye-brain connection

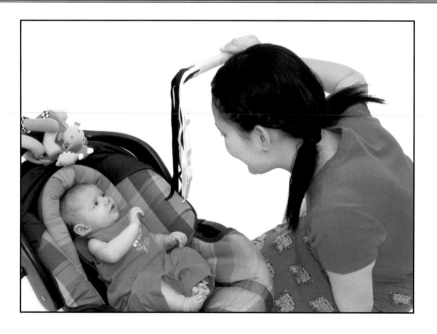

Stimulation of Vision (First and Second month)

❖ In the first two months, babies are able to focus best on black and white because their color vision is still not well developed.

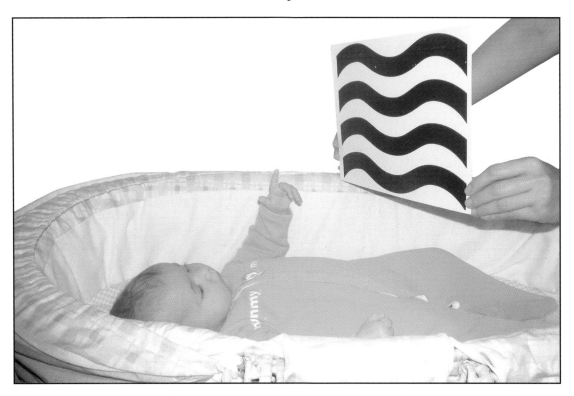

❖ Keep in mind that the baby can only see up to a distance of 13 inches from the face.

❖ Ensure that all the material you present to the baby is within the visual field, Do not forget that the peripheral vision is narrow at this age.

❖ The attention span of a newborn baby can be increased from a few seconds to more than a minute by offering visual stimulation in sharp contrasting black and white patterns.

❖ Newborn babies like to look at complex patterns, and they concentrate on areas of high contrast and edges between shapes and the background. This is one of the reasons why newborns like to look at human faces. They have the ability to recognize the mother's face as early as two days after birth.

ing black and white patterns are recommended to be shown to the baby in
months:

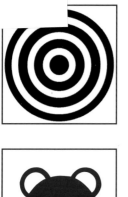   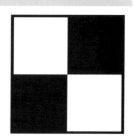

   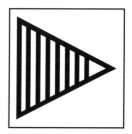

  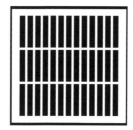 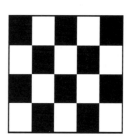

Newborns can best see black and white colors

❖ Hold the Flash Cards in front of the baby's face in the midline.

❖ As you see the baby focusing on the Flash Card, slowly move it about six
inches to the left and then to the right, coming back to the midline.

❖ Now, slowly move the Flash Card upward and downward, coming back to stop again
in the midline at the infant's eye level. Repeat the sequence a few times during the
day.

Tools & Techniques for Visual Stimulation
in the first and second month

Techniques:

Begin communication with your face close and within the visual field of the baby.

Once you have the baby's attention, hold a black and white toy and move it within the visual field, up and down and left to right. Help the baby to track and follow the toy by talking to her at the same time.

Place a black and white crib mobile close enough for the baby to bat it with her arms and legs.

Large crib toys in black and white should be placed in the crib to constantly stimulate vision as well as large motor movements.

Small crib toys and sound-producing wrist rattles will help stimulate vision and grasp.

Objectives:

Stimulates:

Tracking and focusing of the eyes.

Eye/hand coordination.

Muscle movements.

Grasp.

243

Technique:
A crib mirror should be placed in the cot. Babies concentrate and get excited by looking at their image in the mirror.

Objectives:
Emotional development.
Visual and motor skills.
Self-confidence.

Technique:
A black and white picture of the mother, 8x10 inches in size should be placed in the cot. Babies recognize their mothers' faces from the first few days of life. Looking at the mother's face is very comforting for the baby.

Objectives:
Self-confidence.
Emotional development.
Sense of security.

Technique:
Change the position of the crib in the room every few days. Moving it even a few inches or changing the angle gives the baby a different perspective of the surroundings and location.

Objectives:
Visual skills.
Social development.
Cognitive skills.

Technique:
Crib linen with contrasting black and white patterns is highly recommended. Change the linen often enough so the baby sees different patterns on a regular basis. Babies get bored looking at the same objects over and over and love to see different patterns and shapes.

Objectives:
Recognition of patterns, shapes and colors.
Visual stimulation.
Eye/hand coordination.

Tools & Techniques for
Visual Stimulation in the third month

Now that the baby is 3 months old, the vision is improving at a very brisk pace. The baby can focus well at this age, and can clearly see objects within a distance of 10 feet.

Color vision is improving rapidly, and the infant has also gained control of the head and neck.

Do not decorate the room according to your choice of colors. The room should be brightly painted with possibly a different color on each wall. The hangings on the walls should be switched around very frequently.

Have you also thought of the ceiling? Do not forget that the baby spends a lot of time gazing up at the ceiling. The ceiling should be decorated with colorful decorations such as kites, hanging toys or streamers. Also remember to change them around as often as possible.

Technique:
Place the baby in a baby gym with colorful hangings and encourage her to bat at them with the hands and kick with the legs. Change the gym toys very often or the baby will get bored and lose interest.
Objectives:
Vision.
Motor movements.
Eye/hand coordination.
Cause and effect.

Technique:	Technique:
Place a crib mobile within arm and leg batting range of the baby, with highly contrasting, colored patterns. The mobile should have sound-producing toys, as well.	Large crib toys in black and white and other contrasting colors should be placed in the crib.

Objectives:
❖ Vision. ❖ Hearing. ❖ Motor movements.
❖ Recognition of shapes, colors and patterns.

Techniques:
❖ Tie a multicolored toy to a string, hang it within the baby's visual field and move it in a half circle from left to right and vice versa. Start from the midline and go up toward the top of the head and then down toward the chest.

❖ Tie multicolored toys to a stick and place them across the baby's cot within arm batting range of the baby. Change the toys often.

Objectives:
❖ Head and neck control.
❖ Coordination of eyes. ❖ Eye/hand coordination.

<u>Technique</u>:
Visual tracking skills are also very well stimulated by floating balloons over the baby's cot.
The balloons can also be tied to the wrist of the baby.

<u>Objectives</u>:
Vision.
Motor movements.
Cause and effect.

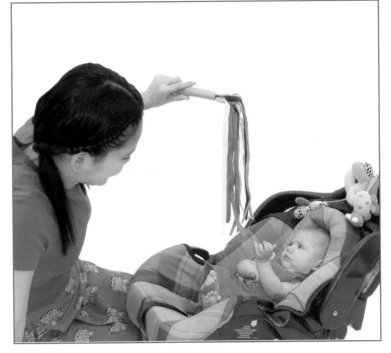

<u>Technique</u>:
Take a stick and tie a few ribbons in different colors to one end of the stick and wave them in front of the baby's face, making verbal sounds at the same time to excite the baby.

<u>Objectives</u>:
Head and neck control.
Vision and hearing.
Vocalizing skills.
Emotional development.

Technique:

● Bring a large multicolored toy from across the room, making verbal communication as you approach the baby. Bring it close and encourage her to reach out and grab the toy.

Objectives:
● Motor movement and coordination.
● Emotional development. ● Communication.

By 2 months of age babies can recognize colors

Technique:

Now that the baby is 3 months old, crib linen should now be colorful with lots of striking patterns and colors, including black and white. Keep changing the linen often. Remember, babies get bored looking at the same patterns and love the change.

Objectives:
Recognition of patterns.
shapes and colors.
Vision.
Eye/hand coordination.

Technique:

A very important step in enhancing the visual, emotional and social development of the infant is interaction with nature. Take the baby outdoors, or if that is not possible, create a small garden area in one corner of the house. Place a small tree over a piece of artificial grass, have some stuffed animals in the area, build a small bird nest with a few eggs in it. Sit with the baby in this area for a while during the day and make intelligent conversation.

Objectives:

Emotional and social development.
Cognitive skills.
Language and speech.
Enhancement of all vital senses.

✋Touch Stimuli

The sense of touch is one of the baby's most advanced faculties at the time of birth.

A newborn is sensitive to the touch from head to toe. Five areas of the body are highly-sensitive. They are the face, palms of the hands, soles of the feet, spinal cord and the genital areas.

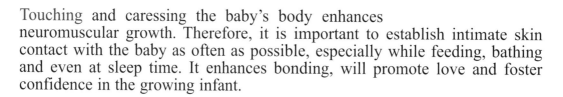

Stroking and caressing the baby stimulates development of the neural pathway. It will also promote myelination process of the nerves.

The myelination process is vital for the nerves to relay messages and transmit information.

Touching and caressing the baby's body enhances neuromuscular growth. Therefore, it is important to establish intimate skin contact with the baby as often as possible, especially while feeding, bathing and even at sleep time. It enhances bonding, will promote love and foster confidence in the growing infant.

Exercise:

* Undress and sit the baby in your lap in front of a large mirror.

* Point out the body parts by touching and naming them, starting from the top of the head down to the feet.

* Touch the baby's skin with different textures, coarse and smooth, hard and soft, even and uneven, naming the textures as you go along.

Smell Stimuli

- Smell plays a vital role in the early emotional development of the baby. It is through smell that the newborn establishes bonding with the mother right from the very first minute of life.

- A newborn baby is an absolute expert at recognizing the odor of her own mother's breast milk.

- It is the sense of smell that helps the infant locate the mother's breast to satisfy her hunger.

Exercise:

To sharpen the sense of smell of your newborn, apply your perfume or body lotion on a cotton ball and wave it under the infants nostrils few times a day. The same should be repeated with cologne or aftershave lotion of the father.

Place your night clothing in the baby's cot. The smell of the parent's clothing is very comforting to the baby. It builds a feeling of security and promotes emotional bonding in the baby.

Expose your baby to pleasing smells, including various foods being cooked in the kitchen. This enhances and develops the connection between the nose and the brain.

Offer a range of different smells to sharpen the baby's sense of smell. It is a good idea to introduce the baby to the different aromatherapy oils during bathing or massage. Do not be afraid to expose the baby even to pungent odors, as all smells are helpful in sharpening this important sense.

Hearing Stimuli

Hearing is a very important sense for a newborn baby. Without a proper sense of hearing, the intellect will not develop and, consequently, speech and language will be impaired.

All babies love to hear human voices and are quite capable of differentiating their mother's voice from that of another person as early as three days of age.

Exercise:

- Infants can easily recognize their parent's voice. It is advisable to record the parent's voice having a conversation with the baby and play it when the parent is at work or unavailable to the baby. This keeps the bonding between the infant and parents well established even when they are not physically together.

- As you know, the mother's heartbeat was the first sound the baby heard and got familiar with. It is most beneficial to play a recording of the mother's heart sounds to the baby when she is irritable or sick.

- Stimulate the hearing of the newborn with different sounds, using rattles and bells.

- Remember, your infant is still learning how to localize the source of the sound, so be gentle and patient. The baby can hear well, so do not be loud. Loud noises can startle and irritate babies.

- Talking to the baby and singing rhymes and lullabies is an intelligent way of stimulating hearing.

- Playing music to the baby stimulates hearing and enhances the IQ.

Speech & Language Stimuli

Babies can hear while in the mother's womb. The hearing of a newborn is very well developed, and we can safely assume that what the newborn hears will register on her growing brain.

Language is made up of sounds, and these basic sounds are called phonemes.

Phonemes are different in every language, and that is the reason why all languages sound different.

Phonemes are stored like sound tracks in the brain. It is therefore important that babies are exposed to good quality language sounds from the beginning of their lives.

Research by Dr. Janallen Huttchenlocher has proved that the size of a toddler's vocabulary is directly related to the amount of communication between the baby and the mother.

If you talk a lot to your baby, by the time she is 20 months of age, she will speak 131 more words than babies who have not been exposed to a lot of language during the same time period.

At the age of two years, the baby's word power will suddenly increase to about 295 words. This is the reason why all parents are advised to talk to their babies in good and complete sentences as much as they can.

The sound of your language is the sound that the baby loves to hear most. Children exposed to good language are more intelligent and have a higher IQ later on in life.

Babies learn by listening to the language spoken around them. The more words they hear, the faster they learn to speak.

At about two months babies start to produce cooing sounds. When your baby coos, respond and participate actively with the baby in the same sounds. This encourages the baby to communicate and helps in acquiring early and good language skills.

I therefore urge you to be an active participant during this phase of your baby's speech development.

The speech and language skills of your baby will depend on the following three important factors:

Your communication technique ⇨

⇨The quality of communication ⇨

⇨The quantity of language.

Your communication technique

Keep your tone soft and loving and look directly into the baby's eyes and face while talking. Keep yourself within the visual field of the baby.

Use meaningful facial expressions, movements of the eyes and movements of the mouth and lips. Even very small babies understand and react to the emotion in your voice. Babies know the difference of being talked to with love and care or being shouted at.

The tone of your voice and the manner in which you speak to the baby has a lot to do with the emotional makeup of the baby's personality.

Interaction while communicating with your baby is essential in stimulating the development of language skills.

The quality of communication

Your quality of communication is also very important and has a great impact on the child's speech and language development. There should be continuity in your language, a descriptive manner and a slow rhythm.

It is beneficial to start using descriptive language even from this early age. For example, while talking about an object to the baby, talk about the size, color, shape and other details. Give as much information as possible in continuous language and complete words.

The style of communication, even from this early age, has a great impact on the speech and language of the baby. When talking to the baby, use sentences in a question form rather than making a statement. Instead of saying, "Come and have your cereal." I would suggest you say, "Would you like to have your cereal now?"

Talking to the baby in this manner is asking for the baby's opinion and inviting her to share in the thought process and decision making. This encourages her sense of participation, and is of great use in emotional development.

The quantity of language.

As an intelligent parent, use all available opportunities to communicate with the baby. Take advantage of feeding time, bathing and changing times, and while carrying out any other day-to-day activities with the baby.

The more you talk, the more information you give to the baby. The more language you use, the larger the base you will provide for your baby's vocabulary and eventual language development.

It is strongly recommended that you start reading storybooks and singing nursery rhymes and lullabies to your baby from the age of two months.

Almost all infant educators are firm and unanimous in their views that early introduction to reading is extremely beneficial for speech and language development, and for the level of intelligence of the baby.

When you read a book to the infant, you are greatly stimulating the sense of vision, hearing, touch, perception, thought process and continuity of language.

Although babies by virtue of nature are preprogrammed for language acquisition, nurturing this ability by intelligent parenting and providing a rich social environment will determine the eventual outcome of this important talent.

Remember, good language skills will also stimulate the development of all the other vital senses of the brain.

For more details please refer to the chapter on Speech & Language

Music Stimuli

There are many benefits of exposing babies to music.

We all know that singing traditional lullabies has a very comforting and soothing effect on a baby.

The first sound a baby hears in the womb is the mother's heartbeat.

Infants therefore prefer to listen to music that is at about 60 to 70 beats per minute, which is roughly the rate at which the mother's heart was beating while the baby was in the mother's womb.

Babies exposed to music have enhanced calculating abilities

It is highly recommended that you play classical music and other forms of soft music to the baby a few times every day.

Benefits of listening to Music

- Music has a calming effect on the developing mind and the brain of the fetus in the womb, and can help shape the emotional component of an infant's personality.

- Babies exposed to music from the time they are in the mother's womb are generally born happy, healthy and relaxed babies.

- Music enhances motor development with the result that babies sit, crawl, stand and walk earlier.

- Music improves language skills. Babies who are exposed and stimulated by music are able to learn to read and write early.

- Babies exposed to classical music are good with numbers, calculation and have good mathematical skills.

- Music develops and enhances the ability to memorize and also helps to increase creative skills.

- Children exposed to music are better learners and tend to have a higher IQ later on, compared to other children of the same age group who have not been exposed to music in early life.

For more details please refer to the chapter on Magical Music.

Motor Skills in the First Quarter

It is a well known fact that a newborn baby's Motor Development progresses from the head downward to the toes.

In the first year of life, the baby goes through the process of Motor Development in the following order:

1. Lifting the head and raising the shoulders

2. Twisting the torso and rolling over

3. Sitting up

4. Crawling

5. Standing

6. Walking

Using Masyog routines enhances physical capabilities and helps babies to achieve milestones faster.

It is not only a question of being able to sit, crawl or walk early, but a matter of encouraging the baby to explore her surroundings continually.

Reaching milestones earlier will lead to greater development in the skills of all the other important vital senses.

Stronger babies are healthier and happier and are bound to be more intelligent and capable in the future.

Stimulation Techniques for
Large Motor Movements

It is advisable to actively stimulate the development and the strength of the large muscle groups of the body from the second month onward. The baby's muscle power and muscle tone have been improving continuously and she is now ready to start exploring her surroundings.

Technique:

To improve head and neck control, place the baby on her tummy with a soft small pillow or cushion under the chest supporting the upper body. This position encourages the baby to lift her neck and head, using the arms as support.

Objectives:
Head, neck and back control.
Strengthens arms and shoulders.
Motor coordination.

☙❧

Technique:

With the baby lying on her tummy and a cushion under her chest, establish eye contact, verbal communication and encourage her to move forward.
Place the palm of your hand against the soles of her feet and help her propel forward.

Objectives:

Motor development.
Leg coordination.
Communication skills.

❧❧

Technique:

Place the baby on the tummy supported by a 'C' cushion with a colorful toy within the visual field.
Move the toy slowly in different directions and angles. Constant verbal communication helps retain the baby's interest in the routine being followed.

Objectives:

Head, neck and back control.
Eye/hand coordination.
Communication skills.

Techniques:

❖ Place the baby on an air-filled cushion with her chest resting on the cushion. Roll the baby forward and backward on the cushion.

❖ Place the baby on her back on the air cushion. Holding the baby at the ankles and the feet, roll her upward and downward.

Objectives:
Head, neck and back control.

Balancing.

Motor development.

The Critical Window of opportunity for Motor development starts from the 5th month.

Stimulation Techniques for
Fine Motor Movements

The stimulation of fine motor movements essentially means that we are trying to stimulate and improve the use of hands and fingers and coordinate their movements.

Techniques:

o In the first few weeks of life, because of involuntary reflex action, babies keep their hands closed in a tight fist. It is a good idea to place rattles with slim handles in the hands of infants.

o Gently open the hands and tickle the palms, and also rub different textures on the palms.

o Open and close the baby's hands and fingers and stroke them gently. When you leave the hand, the baby will close her fist again.

o Around the third month the baby is beginning to acquire control over her movements. It is essential to offer her small toys of various textures, shapes and sizes.

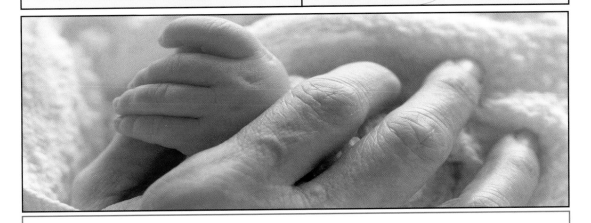

Objectives:
Change of involuntary grasp reflex into voluntary reflex.
Coordination of hand and fingers.
Stimulate sensory pathway.
Recognition of different textures and surfaces.

C8∞

Masyog
Massage and Yoga in the First Quarter

- Masyog is a combination of massage and yoga practice in your baby's life.

- Masyog not only makes bones and joints stronger, but also affects the entire well-being of the mind, soul and body of the infant.

- There is no particular time of the day that could be called the best time for a massage. Do it at the convenience of yourself and the baby. Ensure that the environment is well lit, warm and comfortable for both you and your baby.

Caution:

I would like to stress that concerns for safety are extremely important in any manoeuvre involving physical handling of the baby, especially if the baby has a medical condition. Please seek the advice of your doctor before starting any kind of physical exercise for the baby.

- Before starting, you must establish verbal communication with your baby.
- It is advisable to use oil for the massage, like baby oil or olive oil.
- Yoga stretches should follow soon after the massage, because the muscles are warm and relaxed.

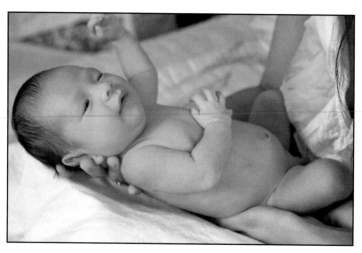

For all the detailed routines please refer to the chapter on Masyog

Balancing & Rocking

- Rocking and Balancing routines stimulate the development of the vestibular apparatus in the inner ear. This will enhance the early development of motor skills and milestones.

- The vestibular stimulation also has a positive effect on the development of emotional and other cognitive abilities of the growing infant.

- Most of the techniques of balancing and rocking are not recommended in the first two months after birth. The reason is that babies are fairly fragile and small during this period.

- A few techniques that can be practiced at this stage, however, are as follows: One simple way to stimulate the vestibular apparatus in an infant under three months of age, is to place him in a small blanket, and holding the blanket by the four corners, sway and rock the baby to and fro.

- Another good exercise for the stimulation of the vestibular apparatus is to hold the baby against your chest while you are sitting on a rocking chair and rock gently.

Rocking and balancing routines stimulate the development of the vestibular apparatus in the inner ear.

Balancing & Rocking
Third Month

Now that your baby is three-months old, you will notice that her head and neck control have improved a lot, and the baby has grown not only in size but has also gained a lot of strength.

It is also a good time to start practicing balancing and rocking techniques in detail.

Upward and downward movements
Backward and forward movement
Sideways swings
Half circle swings
Rocking to and fro
Spinning
Knee balancing
Head down position

For more details please refer to the chapter on Balancing and Rocking.

Stimulation of the Right Brain
First Quarter

Right Brain Stimulation begins from the Third Month.

Objectives of Right Brain Stimulation

Image visualization

High-speed mass memorization (Photographic Memory)

High-speed processing of information

The key is to present large pieces of information at a very rapid rate for the stimulation of the right brain.

Prerequisites of Right Brain Stimulation

Stimulation should only be carried out when the baby is receptive. The baby should be relaxed, well fed and well rested. Providing stimulation to an unhappy baby will result in rejection, agitation and an irritable mother and infant.

The baby and the mother should both be in a comfortable position, preferably seated facing each other.

The surroundings should be pleasant and quiet, without distractions to the mother and the child.The television should not be on, nor should other older children be playing, running around or making a noise in the room.

The area where the stimulation program is being carried out should be well lit and bright.

The Flash Cards that will be used in the program should be of the right size with information printed clearly on them.

- The speed at which the Flash Cards are presented to the infant forms the basis of this exercise.

- The Flash Cards are presented very rapidly at the rate of one card per second.

- Remember clearly that the cards are not being shown for memorization; rather the speed at which they are being shown is serving as a stimulus for the right brain.

- By presenting the Flash Cards at a great speed, we are trying to develop the imaging and the photographic capability of the right brain.

- Also remember that by presenting the cards rapidly we are helping the mass memorization and the high speed processing faculties of the right brain.

- If we were to present these cards at a slow rate, we would be stimulating the left brain which, as we know, works as a slow-speed computer. In such case, the right brain would remain inactive, and we would be defeating the purpose of our exercise.

The Flash Card presentation sessions should be brief. Long sessions will lead to a lack of concentration on the part of the infant and defeat the purpose of the program.

Do not repeat the same set of Flash Cards over and over again. Keep changing the sequence of the cards. The mind of the infant is more receptive to new and fresh knowledge all the time.

Sequence of the Flash Cards

Following is the chart for the Flash Cards that will be used in the third month.

They have been grouped into different categories to be presented to the infant in an orderly routine.

Category	Number of Flash cards	Type
Animals	Four	Any four animals
Fruits and Vegetables	Four	Any four fruits and vegetables
Colors	Three	Red, blue and yellow
Alphabets	Five	A to E
Common Objects	Four	Any four objects
Shapes	Three	Circle, triangle and square
Numbers	Four	1 to 4
Dots	Five	Cards with 1 - 5 dots

In the third month, we will be showing a total of 32 Flash Cards.

It is also advisable, once in a while, to show the black and white Flash Cards which were used in the first two months.

To make it even easier for the parent/caregiver or the program instructor, the categories have been divided into two groups of 16 Flash Cards each. Group I and Group 2 are shown on different days of the week as outlined in the schedule that follows.

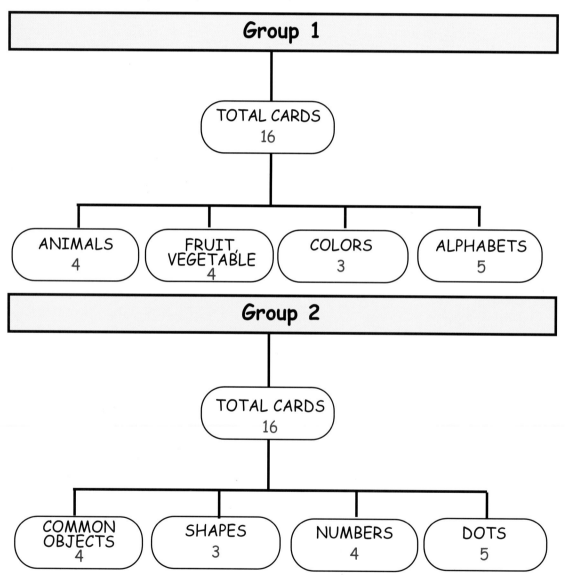

Group 1

TOTAL CARDS
16

| ANIMALS 4 | FRUIT, VEGETABLE 4 | COLORS 3 | ALPHABETS 5 |

Group 2

TOTAL CARDS
16

| COMMON OBJECTS 4 | SHAPES 3 | NUMBERS 4 | DOTS 5 |

Schedule for the presentation of the Flash Cards

Day	Group
Monday	Group 1
Tuesday	Group 2
Wednesday	Group 1
Thursday	Group 2
Friday	Group 1
Saturday	Group 2
Sunday	Group 1

❖ As stressed earlier, the Flash Cards have to be shown rapidly at the rate of one card per second.

❖ There are no hard and fast rules for the order of showing the Flash Cards. In the first few sessions, you might want to follow a pattern to get the baby familiar with the program. Once the routine is set, it is advisable to keep changing the sequence.

❖ Pick the required number of cards from the different categories. Keep changing the cards often. For example, if you showed apple, orange, banana and carrot on a given day, then in the next session you might want to show melon, strawberry, grape and cucumber. Change keeps the baby's mind fresh and receptive.

❖ In the case of the "Dot Cards" It is recommended to follow a sequence for at least a few weeks in the beginning. Once you are confident that the baby is concentrating and responding well, you might want to try a random sequence.

❖ Dot cards are very important for the development of counting and calculating abilities of the right brain.

❖ You can show the baby all the cards in a single session, but it is recommended that you take a short break between different categories. This helps the baby to retain interest and concentration.

> The Flash Card sequence should be repeated twice every day.

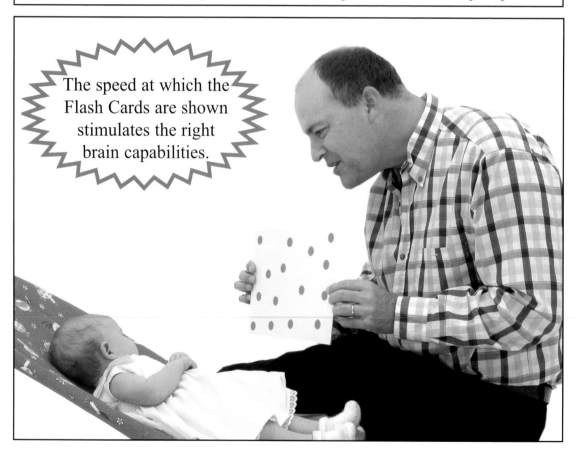

The speed at which the Flash Cards are shown stimulates the right brain capabilities.

❧

Stimulation Program in the Second Quarter

Fourth, fifth and sixth month

❧

* To refrain from being biased toward the gender of babies 'She' and 'He' have been used in alternate chapters and quarters of the program.

* To emphasize the importance of stimulation, a few techniques have been repeated in all quarters .

Do not forget that the baby is approaching the stage of th
opportunity. This is when, one by one, the important vital s
hearing, and touch are going to have the opportunity to develo
stimuli they receive. Because of these windows of opportunity ope
the development of the brain going on at such a rapid rate, the first y
critical time in the development of your baby. Poor quality stimulatio
have an irreversible effect on the intelligence of the baby.
At this stage, the right brain is functionally more active than the left b.
brain is the one that has the special ability for photographic memo   mass
memorization. This ability can be developed by showing the Flash Cards a. a rapid rate
and in large numbers.

✆ More Facts To Remember

* Genetics play a fairly important part in determining the intelligence of an individual. However, a greater role in determining the eventual intelligence and the capabilities of the brain depends on how the brain is being nurtured.

* After the age of 18 months, the connections that are not being used will start to fade away and die. Connections that are being nourished, nurtured and being reinforced will flourish.

* The critical window for the sense of vision will be wide open between 4 to 8 months of age. This is a very valuable time for maximum stimulation of vision.

* The critical window for the sense of hearing is open for opportunities from 4 months of age to about 10 months of age.

* Critical windows have to be recognized and appreciated because once closed shut, they will never open again.

* By the age of 4 months, the visual capability of an infant is comparable to that of an adult.

* Touching and caressing the baby speeds up motor development.

* The right brain is more dominant than the left brain in the first 3 years of life. Children lose their ability to use the right brain after the first 6 years. It is therefore critical to stimulate the right brain earlier on.

The Second Quarter Program

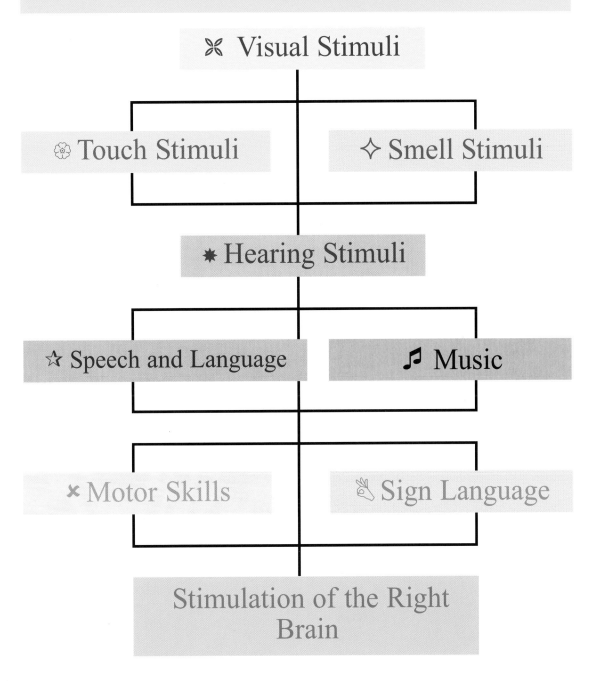

✖ Visual Stimuli

✿ Touch Stimuli   ✧ Smell Stimuli

✴ Hearing Stimuli

☆ Speech and Language   ♪ Music

✖ Motor Skills   ✌ Sign Language

Stimulation of the Right Brain

Vision Stimulation in the Second Quarter

Objectives of Visual Stimulation

* Stimulate and increase concentration

* Stimulate the tracking and focusing abilities of the eyes

* Stimulate coordination of the eyes

* Stimulate the movements of the head and neck

* Stimulate eye/hand coordination

* Stimulate and enrich the eye/brain connection

Since your baby is 4 months old at this time, vision and the recognition of colors are improving at a very rapid pace. This is a good time to stimulate the baby's visual sense to the maximum.

Tools & Techniques for
Visual Stimulation

All the stimulation techniques that we used in the first three months will be followed in the same way with the addition of new techniques.

Techniques:

- Continue stimulation with a crib mobile within reach of the baby's arms, and legs. It should have highly contrasting, colored patterns.
- Continue with the balloon technique.
- Continue with the technique of multicolored toy tied to a string and hung within the visual field.

Objectives:

Visual stimulation.
Motor movements.
Color recognition.
Cause and effect.

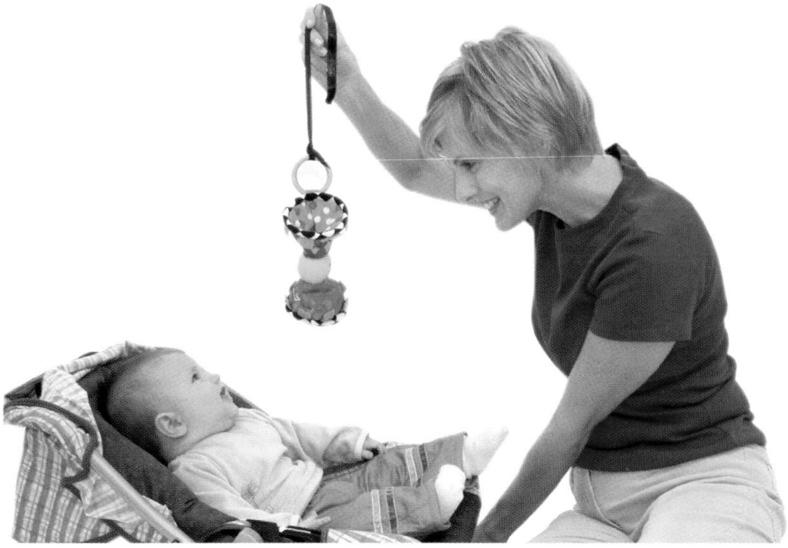

<u>**Techniques**</u>:

❖ Continue with the ribbons tied to a stick technique.

❖ Continue stimulating the baby with the large multicolored toy and verbal communication.

❖ With the baby lying on his back, place a large soft toy or the palms of hands against the baby's feet and encourage him to kick.

❖ Continue with the mirror in the crib technique.

Objectives:

Head and neck control.
Vision.
Hearing.
Communication skills.
Eye/hand coordination.
Eye/foot coordination.

<u>**Techniques**</u>:

❊ This is an excellent time to start with the ever-favorite peek-a-boo.

❊ Continue placing a black and white picture of the mother in the crib.

❊ Keep changing the position of his crib in the room.

❊ Crib blankets and crib sheets should be colorful with lots of striking patterns and colors.

Objectives:
Object permanence.
Sense of security.
Cognitive skills.
Emotional development.

Techniques:

- Place the baby in your lap and bring a toy close to him within his reach. Keeping his attention on the toy, drop it on the floor or in a bucket and express your surprise verbally. Encourage him to look for the toy on the floor or in the bucket.
- Place a toy in each of the baby's hands and encourage him to hold on to the toys individually.

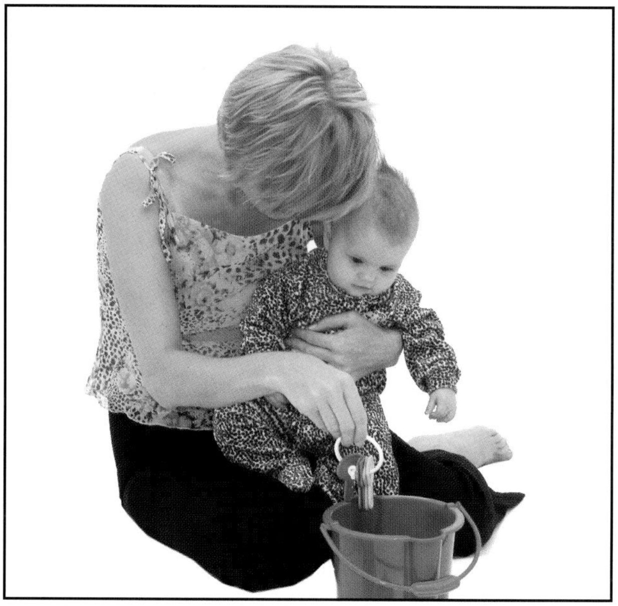

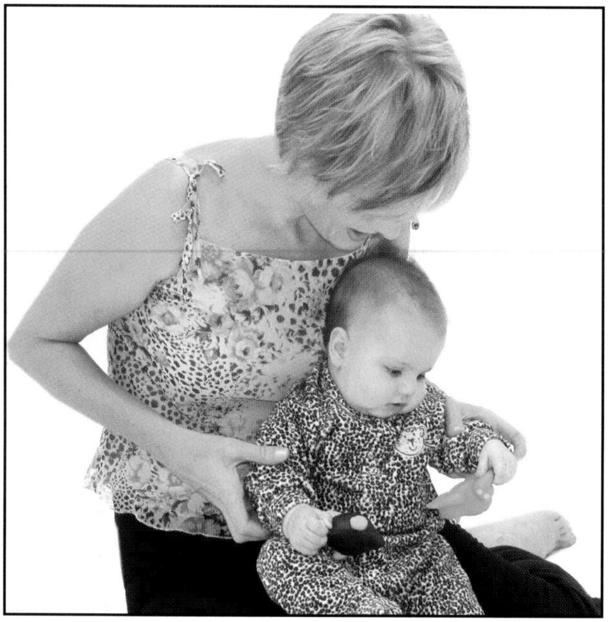

Objectives:

Vision
Eye/hand coordination.
Bilateral hand coordination.
Recognition of surfaces and textures.

Technique:

As soon as his head control is good you will find that the baby is very observant and looks around with interest. Take him for a stroll to the playground and let him interact with nature and his surroundings. Leave him on the grass, and show him the trees, flowers, birds and people around him. Point out clouds, the sky, flowerbeds, flying birds and other pet animals around. Make intelligent and interesting conversation with the baby.

Objectives:

Social and emotional development.

Cognitive skills.

Speech and language.

Enhancement of all vital senses.

The tools and techniques for the following stimuli remain the same as have been followed in the previous quarter.

Touch
Stimuli

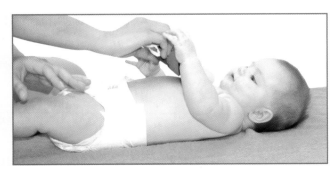

Smell

Stimuli

Hearing

Stimuli

Speech and Language Stimuli

Music Stimuli ♪

For more details please refer to the corresponding chapters.

Motor Skills

Large Motor Movements

Stimulation of the large muscle groups is much easier and a lot of fun at this stage, because the baby is bigger and has gained good muscle strength and coordination.

Techniques:

- ◆ Continue using the play gym as a stimulation tool.

- ◆ Place the baby on his back on a soft blanket. Hold two corners of the blanket and help the baby to roll over. Practice in both directions.

- ◆ Take a large colorful ball and attach it to a string. Place it in front of the baby's arms and then the legs. Move it in all directions and bring it from far to near.

- ◆ Place the baby in two air-filled rings and encourage him to reach for toys.

- ◆ Place the baby on his tummy with a soft pillow under his chest. Dangle a colored toy within visual field. Move the toy upward and downward. Encourage the baby to raise himself on his arms and follow the movement of the toy.

Objectives:

- ■ Teaches the baby to roll over.
- ■ Balancing.
- ■ Motor development.
- ■ Coordination of movements.
- ■ Head, neck and back control.

Technique:

♦ Continue placing the baby on the 'C' cushion as you did in the first quarter. Establish eye contact, meaningful verbal communication and encourage the baby to propel forward. Place colorful toys within his reach and keep moving them farther and farther as he tries to reach for them.

Objectives:

Head neck and back control.
Motor development and coordination of upper/lower body.
Eye/hand coordination.
Communication skills.
Grasp.

Technique:
■Continue with the technique of placing the baby on the air filled cushion, first on the tummy and then the back. Roll the baby over the cushion in forward and backward direction.

Objectives:
■ Head, neck and back control.
■ Balancing.
■ Motor development.

Fine Motor Movements

<u>Techniques</u>:

❖ Gently open the hands and touch the palms of your baby with different textures.
❖ Place small toys with various shapes and surfaces in the baby's hands and encourage him to hold them and feel them.
❖ While feeding the baby, encourage him to put his hands around the bottle to hold it.
❖ While spoon feeding the baby, let the baby hold the spoon with your help and feed himself.
❖ Introduce and encourage hand play using soft squeaky toys.

<u>Objectives:</u>
Grasp.
Eye/hand coordination.
Touch.

❖ Start with the all-time favorite Jack in the Box, or other pop-up toys.

❖ Begin with the stacking and nesting toys at this stage.

❖ Let the baby play with empty boxes and plastic cups. Encourage him to put his hands inside and explore.

❖ Let the baby beat on a drum, xylophone or hit the piano keys.

❖ Start playing with two-to-four piece puzzles. In the beginning you will have to show it a few times before the baby starts to develop interest in this play.

Objectives:

❖ Cause and effect. ❖ Shape and size discrimination.

❖ Hand/finger coordination

❖ Eye/hand coordination. ❖ Problem solving.

Technique:

Take a large picture of a baby. Identify the various parts of the body on the picture and at the same time touch and identify your baby's body parts.

Objectives:

Self recognition.

Emotional development.

Masyog
(Massage and Yoga)

Follow the same routines for Massage and Yoga stretches as per the first quarter with increased range of stretches, as your baby now has more muscle power.

Balancing and Rocking

For more details please refer to the chapters on 'Masyog' and 'Balancing & Rocking'.

Sign ✋ Language

The signs that are recommended are based on the American Sign Language (ASL) system. These are standardized and most widely used.

Many parents develop and use their own signs. You can use any sign that helps the baby to communicate as long as you are consistent.

PREREQUISITES FOR SIGNING

It is important to use the right sign at the right time, and correlate it to the appropriate activity. For example, teach the sign for milk just before giving the bottle to the baby. Similarly, teach the flower sign while out in the park or garden.

Be consistent with the signs. If you use a different sign for the same word on different occasions, the baby will get confused.

Repetition and reinforcement is extremely important. The more you use a particular sign, the easier it becomes for the baby to learn it.

When you feel the baby may have learned to recognize the sign, encourage the baby to participate by repeating the sign back to you.

Use a lot of vocal language and facial expressions when signing with the baby.

Do not look for immediate results, or both you and the baby will get frustrated. Remember, it will take some time for the baby to learn what is going on. Once the baby has learned a few signs, it gets easier to pick up more and more signs. Have patience and make the sign language a happy game for yourself and your baby.

It may be some time before the baby will start signing back. A good time to start signing with your baby is around six months of age.

A few of the common signs that are recommended in this quarter are as follows:

Milk

☞ Milk - Open and close the hand a few times as if milking a cow.

Eat

☞ Eat - Point the fingers and thumb toward the mouth.

Drink

☞ Drink - As if holding a glass, place the thumb at the lower lip. Tilt the head backward to signify drinking action.

More

☞ More - The fingers and the thumb of both hands are held together and tapped at the tips a few times.

Change	Water

⮜ Change - Place one fist against the other at chest level and move at the knuckles in opposite directions.	⮜ Water - The thumb and the little finger are held together with the other fingers stretched out. Tap the angle of the mouth with the index finger.

For more details please refer to the chapter on Sign Language.

Stimulation of the Right Brain
Second Quarter

Objectives of
Right Brain Stimulation

Image visualization

High-speed mass memorization (Photographic Memory)

High-speed processing of information

Prerequisites for the Right Brain Stimulation are the same as the previous quarter

Sequence of the Flash Cards

Following is the chart for the **Flash Cards** that will be used in the fourth, fifth and sixth Month.

They have been grouped into different categories to be presented to the infant in an orderly routine.

Category	Number of Flash cards	Type
Animals	Ten	Any Ten animals
Fruits and Vegetables	Ten	Any Ten fruits and vegetables
Colors	Six	Red, blue and yellow green, orange & purple
Alphabets	Twelve	A to L
Words	Eight	Any eight words
Common Objects	Ten	Any Ten objects
Shapes	Six	Circle, triangle, square, rectangle, diamond & oval
Numbers	Six	1 to 6
Dots	20	1-20

In the fourth, fifth and the sixth months we will be showing a total number of 88 cards.

These flash cards are inclusive of the thirty-two flash cards that we used in the first three months.

To make it even easier for the parent/care giver or the program instructor, the categories have been divided into two groups Group 1 contains 46 flash cards and group 2 contains 42 flash cards.

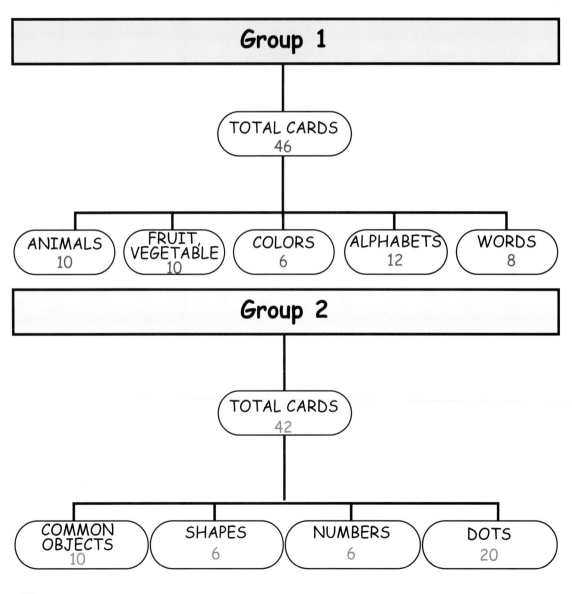

Schedule for the presentation of the
Flash Cards

Day	Group
Monday	Group 1
Tuesday	Group 2
Wednesday	Group 1
Thursday	Group 2
Friday	Group 1
Saturday	Group 2
Sunday	Group 1

❖ As has been stressed earlier, the Flash Cards have to be shown rapidly at the rate of one card per second.

❖ There are no hard and fast rules about showing the cards in any specific order. In the first few sessions, you might want to follow a pattern to get the baby familiar with the program. Once the routine is set, it is advisable to keep changing the sequence.

❖ Pick the required number of cards from the different categories. Change the cards often. Change keeps the baby's mind fresh and receptive.

❖ In the case of the "Dot Card," it is advisable to follow a sequence for at least a few weeks in the beginning. Once you are confident that the baby is concentrating and responding well, you might want to try a random sequence.

❖ Dot Cards are very important for the development of counting and the calculating abilities of the right brain.

❖ You can show the baby all the cards in a single session, but it is recommended that you take a short break between different categories. This helps the baby to retain interest and concentration.

❖ Looking at our table, we know that on Monday we will be using Flash Cards from Group1:

    10 animals
    10 fruits & vegetable
     6 colors
    12 alphabets
     8 words
    Total of 46 flash cards.

❖ Similarly, on Tuesday, we will be showing Flash Cards from Group 2:

   10 common Objects
    6 shapes
    6 numbers
  20 dots.
Total of 42 Flash Cards.

The Flash Card sequence should be repeated twice every day.

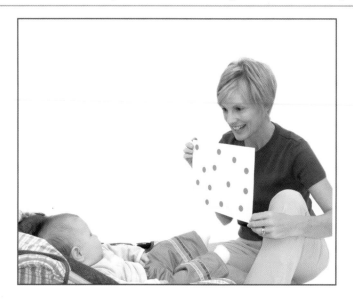

Stimulation Program in the Third Quarter

Seventh, eighth and ninth month

* To refrain from being biased toward the gender of babies 'She' and 'He' have been used in alternate chapters and quarters of the program.

* To emphasize the importance of stimulation, a few techniques have been repeated in all quarters .

Your baby is already six-months old and the next three months are the most exciting months for both the baby and yourself. Till now, the baby was totally dependent on you, whereas now she has begun to move around and is ready to become the great explorer of the world around her.

Your baby's vision has improved dramatically by this time, and also the motor movements are much more synchronized. The hearing is sharper, and the language expressions and communication are beginning to take a meaningful shape. The interaction with others and the world around has entered a very interesting phase.

❋ More Facts to Remember ❋

---

* The strength of the trillions of connections that the brain cells form with each other in the first three years determines the quality of the vital senses. Connections are strengthened by their repeated and good use.

* Connections that are nourished, nurtured and reinforced will flourish. After the age of one and a half connections that are not being used will begin to fade away.

* The quality of language and the amount of communication to which babies are exposed is extremely important in the development of vocabulary, speech, and language skills.

* Delay in language development is the most common childhood disability. It affects up to 10 percent or more of all seven-year olds. Imprinting the brain by exposure to high quality language is very important in the first year of life, especially in the first six months.

* Motherese is an effective way of starting communication with the baby. It helps them in language acquisition and emotional development.

* Reading storybooks to infants is an extremely effective tool in promoting the development of language.

The Third Quarter Program

◎ Visual Stimuli

✋ Touch Stimuli

✿ Smell Stimuli

👂 Hearing Stimuli

🗨 Speech and Language

♪ Music

⌘ Motor Skills

👌 Sign Language

Stimulation of the Right Brain

Vision
Stimulation in the seventh, eighth and ninth month

Objectives of Visual Stimulation

* To stimulate and increase concentration.

* To stimulate the tracking and focusing abilities of the eyes.

* To stimulate coordination of the eyes.

* To stimulate the movements of the head and neck.

* To stimulate eye/hand coordination.

* To stimulate and enrich the eye/brain connection.

At seven months of age, your baby's field of vision, eye coordination, color vision and the ability to track are all very well developed. The movements of the muscles are not only getting stronger but the motor coordination is also improving rapidly.

Tools & Techniques for Visual Stimulation

All the stimulation techniques that we used in the earlier programs will be followed in the same routine with the addition of the new ones.

Techniques:

- Continue the exercise of dropping toys on the floor, expressing your surprise and drawing the attention of the baby toward them.

- Take two small toys and place one in the baby's right hand and the other in her left. This is to encourage her to hold an object in each hand.

- Continue with the ever-favorite peek-a-boo play with your baby.

Objectives:

Eye/hand coordination.
Bilateral hand coordination.
Shape and size discrimination.
Object permanence.

Technique:

Taking the baby out to the park, shopping mall and other public places provides her with a good opportunity to interact with people and surroundings.

Objectives:
Social and emotional development.
Cognitive skills.
Speech and language.
Enhancement of all vital senses.

The tools and techniques for the following stimuli remain the same as have been followed in the previous quarter.

Touch Stimuli

Smell Stimuli

Hearing Stimuli

Speech and Language stimuli

Music Stimuli

For details please refer to the corresponding chapters.

Motor Skills

Stimulation of the Large Motor Movements

Your baby is now growing rapidly and is gaining muscle strength. The baby's coordination is getting better, so stimulation of the large muscle groups is easier and more fun as well. The techniques are essentially the same as you have been following till now, and you are encouraged to carry on the Motor Stimulation in the same way.

Techniques:

*Water play and bathing times are other very exciting games at this stage. Put the baby in the bathtub and let him splash around. Use lots of floating and squirting toys of different shapes, forms and sizes. Throw in a few colorful plastic books as well.

Objectives:

* Vision stimulation.   * Eye/hand coordination.
* Motor development and coordination.

Stimulation Of Fine Motor Movements

Techniques:
* Encourage your baby to hold a small toy in one hand and try to pass it to the other.
* Place small toys with various shapes and textures in the baby's hands and encourage him to hold them and feel them.
* Continue encouraging the baby to hold the bottle or the spoon at meal times.
* Continue using soft squeaky toys and encourage hand play.
* Place empty boxes, buckets or plastic cups in front of the baby for him to put his hands inside and explore.

Objectives:

* Grasp.   * Eye/hand coordination.   * Bilateral coordination.
* Touch sensation.

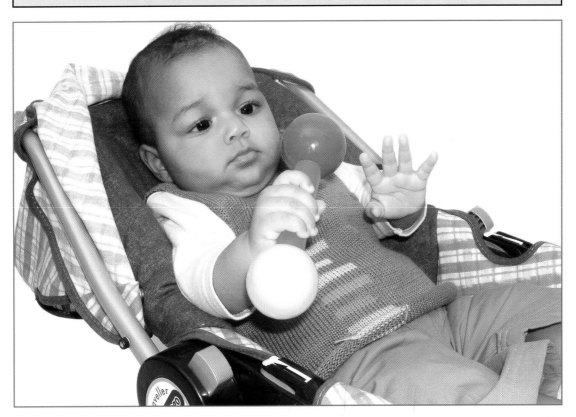

Technique:
☐ Start the hide-and-seek games by hiding toys under sheets and cushions and encourage the baby to look for them.

Objective:
Object permanence.
Eye/hand coordination.

Techniques:
Play with the baby using stacking toys and nesting toys.

☐ Continue with the all-time favorite "Jack in the box."

☐ Start playing with the shape sorters.

☐ Make a small sandbox and put some spoons, plastic cups, a shovel and a few small empty containers in the sand. Let the baby play in the sandbox with these toys.

☐ Encourage the baby to place toys of different sizes and shapes one by one in a large container.

☐ Start playing with four-to-six piece puzzles.

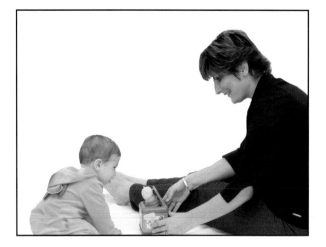

Objectives:

☐ Shape and size discrimination.

☐ Cause and effect.

☐ Eye/hand coordination.

☐ Problem solving.

☐ Touch sensation.

Masyog
Massage and yoga in the third Quarter

☐ Follow the same routines for massage and yoga stretches as in the previous quarter. Continue with the increased range of stretches, as your baby has better muscle power.

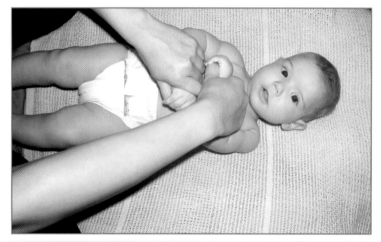

Balancing & Rocking

Since the baby has gained good muscle control, and muscular movements are well coordinated, it makes rocking and balancing a very playful experience.
The Balancing Techniques will also enhance the development of motor skills.

For more details please refer to the chapters on "Masyog" and "Balancing & Rocking."

Sign ✋ Language

Prerequisites for using Sign Language remain the same as the previous quarter with the addition of the following signs

The signs that have been incorporated in this quarter are as follows:

Baby 	**Flower** 
✌ Baby - Place one forearm on top of the other and rock from side to side.	✌ Flower - Holding the fingers and the thumb of the hand together, touch one side of the nose and then the other.
Banana 	**Apple** 
✌ Banana - Place curved index finger of one hand along the straight index finger of the other hand and move up and down.	✌ Apple - Place the curved index finger on the cheek and twist a few times.

Cat 	Dog 
🖑Cat - The index finger and the thumb are held together at the corner of the mouth with the other fingers fanning out.	🖑Dog - The tip of the middle finger and the thumb are held together and snapped a few times.

For more details please refer to the chapter on Sign Language.

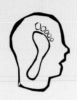

Stimulation of the Right Brain
Third Quarter

Objectives of Right Brain Stimulation

Image visualizatoin

High-speed mass memorization (Photographic Memory)

High Speed processing of information

Prerequisites of right brain stimulation are the same as the previous quarters.

Sequence of the Flash Cards

Following is the chart for the **Flash Cards** that will be used in the seventh, eighth and the ninth month.

They have been grouped into different categories to be presented to the baby in an orderly routine.

Category	Number of Flash cards	Type
Animals	Eighteen	Any eighteen animals
Fruits and Vegetables	Eighteen	Any eighteen fruits and vegetables
Colors	Nine	Red, Blue, Yellow, Green, Orange, Purple, Pink, Brown and Grey
Alphabets	Nineteen	A to S
Words	Sixteen	Any sixteen words
Common Objects	Eighteen	Any eighteen objects
Shapes	Nine	Circle, triangle, square, rectangle, oval, diamond, trapezoid, cross & star
Numbers	Eight	1 to 8
Dots	Thirty Five	1-35 dot cards

In the seventh, eighth and ninth months, we will be showing a total of 150 Flash Cards which are inclusive of the 88 cards from the previous quarters.

To make it even easier for the parent/caregiver or the program instructor, the categories have been divided into two groups.

Group 1 contains 80 Flash Cards, and Group 2 contains 70 Flash Cards.

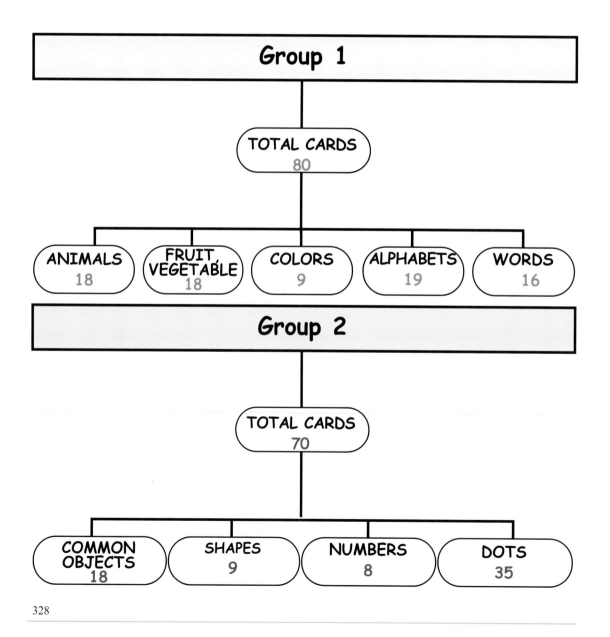

Group 1

TOTAL CARDS
80

| ANIMALS 18 | FRUIT, VEGETABLE 18 | COLORS 9 | ALPHABETS 19 | WORDS 16 |

Group 2

TOTAL CARDS
70

| COMMON OBJECTS 18 | SHAPES 9 | NUMBERS 8 | DOTS 35 |

Schedule for presentation of the
Flash Cards

Day	**Group**
Monday	Group 1
Tuesday	Group 2
Wednesday	Group 1
Thursday	Group 2
Friday	Group 1
Saturday	Group 2
Sunday	Group 1

❖ As stressed earlier, the Flash Cards have to be shown rapidly, at the rate of one card per second.

❖ The cards have to be shown in two sessions through the course of the day.

❖ There are no hard-and-fast rules pertaining to any specific order to show the flash cards. It is advisable to follow a pattern and keep changing the sequence.

❖ In the case of the Dot Cards as well, it is advisable to follow a sequence for at least a few weeks in the beginning. Once you are confident that the baby is concentrating and responding well, you might want to try a random sequence.

❖ Dot cards are very important for the development of counting and calculating abilities of the right brain.

❖ You can show the baby all the cards in a single session, but it is recommended that you take a short break between different categories. This helps the baby to retain interest and concentration.

❖ Looking at our table, we know that on Monday we will be using Flash Cards from Group 1:

18 animals

18 fruits & vegetable

 9 colors

19 alphabets

16 words

Total of 80 Flash cards.

❖ Similarly, on Tuesday we will be showing flash cards from Group 2:

18 common objects

 9 shapes

 8 numbers

35 dots.

Total of 70 Flash Cards.

The Flash Card sequence should be repeated twice every day.

Stimulation Program in the

Fourth Quarter

Tenth, eleventh and twelfth month

* To refrain from being biased toward the gender of babies 'She' and 'He' have been used in alternate chapters and quarters of the program.

* To emphasize the importance of stimulation, a few techniques have been repeated in all quarters .

Your baby is now nine-months old, crawling all over the place, pushing and pulling everything in sight. It takes some effort on your part to try and keep him occupied. The baby now knows very clearly exactly what he wants and will throw a tantrum if things are not going in his favour.

Safety at this stage is of great importance. Make sure there are no sharp edges around the house because the baby is going to be moving around quite freely. Make sure all electrical sockets are covered, with no loose wires or plugs hanging around. Watch out for slippery floors, and do not leave the baby unattended in the washroom.

More Facts to Remember

❖ Stimulation of the left brain will enhance reasoning, logic and mathematics.

❖ Stimulation of the right brain will develop artistic faculties such as music, and intuitive thinking.

❖ It is easy to train and stimulate the brain at the age of four than at five.

❖ It is easier to train and stimulate the brain at the age of three years than at four.

❖ It is much easier to train the brain at the age of two, as compared to the age of three years.

❖ It is easiest of all to train the brain from birth through the first two years of life.

❖ An average 12-month-old baby understands about 55 words, but may speak only one or two. At 16 months, he will understand 170 words and can speak about 25.

❖ Language explosion starts at about 18 months, when a child has a spoken vocabulary of about 50 words and understands about 200 words.

❖ By the time the baby is 24-months old, the vocabulary is more than 200 words of spoken language and an understanding of as many as 1,000 words.

The Fourth Quarter Program

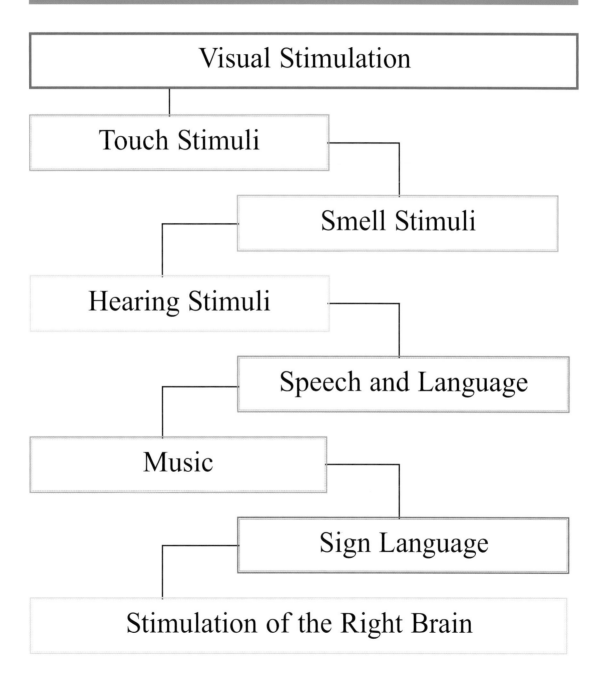

Visual Stimulation

Touch Stimuli

Smell Stimuli

Hearing Stimuli

Speech and Language

Music

Sign Language

Stimulation of the Right Brain

Visual Stimulation

Objectives of Visual Stimulation

¤ To stimulate and increase concentration.

¤ To stimulate the tracking and focusing abilities of the eyes.

¤ To stimulate coordination of the eyes.

¤ To stimulate the movements of the head, neck and the body.

¤ To stimulate eye/hand coordination.

¤ To stimulate and enrich the eye/brain connection.

Between the ages of 10 to 12 month, baby's vision has improved greatly, and the visual acuity will reach 20/20, just like an adult, by the time you are celebrating his first birthday. Now, your baby's field of vision, coordination of the eyes, color vision and the ability to track are all very well developed. By the age of one year, the baby will be moving around, holding on to furniture. He may start to take a few steps without support.

Tools and Techniques for Visual Stimulation

All the same techniques used in the previous quarters will be followed in the same manner with the addition of these new ones:

Techniques:

⇨ Tie a moving toy car or a bus to a long piece of ribbon and encourage the baby to go for it by moving it away from him.

⇨ Take an empty shoe box and show the baby how you put different toys into the box and close the lid. Encourage him to open the box and take the toys out and place them back again.

⇨ Take three of four large balls of different colors and roll them away from the baby in different directions. Encourage the baby to go after the balls. Once he has held a ball ask him to roll the ball to you.

337

⮕ Switch on a colored flashlight and let the baby try to follow the beam of the light as you move it around.

⮕ Hang a wind chime somewhere in the room. Take the baby close to the chime and encourage him to tap it to produce interesting sounds.

⮕ When your baby starts to stand up holding on to the edge of the table, put a toy in front of him and keep moving it farther and farther away as the baby tries to grab it.

Objectives:

⮕   Eye/hand coordination.
⮕   Motor development.
⮕   Balancing.

Techniques:

✍ Sit the baby in a high chair and put a few small toys in front of him. Encourage him to hold the toys first and then drop them on the floor.

✍ Sit the baby in your lap, bring a toy within his reach, and draw his attention to the toy. Keeping his attention on the toy, drop it on the floor and express your surprise verbally. Encourage him to look for the toy on the floor.

Objectives:

Grasp and release.
Eye/hand coordination.
Cause and effect.

Techniques:

✍ Continue with the ever-favorite peek-a-boo.

✍ Let the baby still practice his skills on the drum, xylophone and the piano.

✍ Continue with the all-time favorite Jack in the box and other pop up toys.

Objectives:

Vision.
Cause and effect.
Object permanence.

Technique:

○ Continue interaction with nature and your visits to the parks, playgrounds and public places. Encourage your baby to interact with other children of the same age group. Introduce him to mother and toddler play groups, activity workshops and social gatherings with other children.

Objectives:

○ Social and emotional development.
○ Cognitive skills.
○ Speech and language.
○ Concept of sharing.
○ Enhancement of all vital senses.

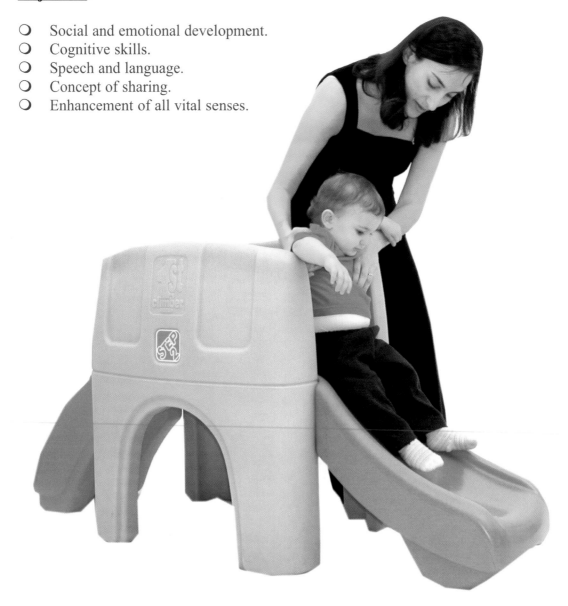

The tools and techniques for the following stimuli remain the same as has been followed in the previous quarters.

Touch Stimuli

Now the baby is fairly mobile and is crawling freely, walking with support and is finding his way around. With all kinds of surfaces and forms to handle, this is a marvelous time to enhance the baby's sense of touch.

Smell Stimuli

Stimulating the sense of smell comes naturally now as the baby keeps growing and is very mobile.

Hearing Stimuli

Stimulation of the sense of hearing comes naturally and easily as the baby is growing up.

Speech and Language Stimuli

Babies learn to speak by listening to the language around them. The quality and quantity of the language therefore becomes an important factor in determining the eventual language skills and vocabulary of the growing baby.

The three important factors that have been stressed all along are:

The Communication Technique

The Quality of Communication

The Quantity of Communication

Music Stimuli

Motor Skills

Stimulation of Large Motor Movements

Now your baby is growing rapidly and is gaining muscle strength. The coordination of movements is getting better, and stimulation of the large muscle groups is easier and a lot of fun as well.

<u>Techniques:</u>

- Once your baby is good at crawling, a good game to play is crawling through the tunnel.

- Place a large colorful beach ball in front of the baby. Stand behind the baby and hold him under the arms and encourage him to kick the ball.

- Put the baby in a large plastic tub filled with small multicolored plastic balls.

- Hold the baby in the upright position. Place his feet over your feet and walk with him.
- Encourage playing on slides and swings.
- Once your baby is comfortable walking with your support, place a few obstacles and teach the baby to walk around them.

- When you feel your baby is starting to crawl well, make a small uneven mountain, using soft floor cushions of different sizes or a bean bag. Vocalize with baby and encourage the baby to climb up and down.

- Continue with the exciting water play at bath times.

- A good tool to use at this age is the upright push walker. Please ensure that all safety measures have been taken.

Objectives:

Vision.
Motor skills.
Body awareness.
Bilateral coordination.
Balancing.
Eye/foot coordination.

Stimulation Of
Fine Motor Movements

The following techniques stimulate the movements and coordination of the hands and fingers.

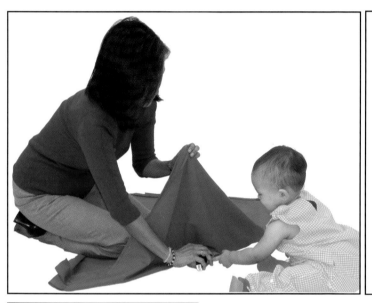

Techniques:

- Continue playing peek-a-boo. When hiding toys, make them slightly more difficult to find as the baby learns the easy hiding places.

- Knead some soft dough and make it into different shapes. Let the baby feel and play with the dough.

- Continue to encourage the baby to hold the bottle and spoon at feeding times.

- Show the baby pictures of siblings and other family members.

- Continue to encourage the baby to place objects in and out of boxes.

●Continue playing with stacking and nesting toys.

- Continue to encourage the baby to play with shape sorters.

- This is a good time to start playing with finger paints. Place some paints in a platter and spread out a big white sheet of paper on the floor. Help your child dabble with the paints and smear on the paper.

- Continue to encourage sand box play involving siblings and other children of the same age group.

- Encourage the baby to sit around with friends and siblings and play with six-to-eight piece puzzles.

Objectives:

Object permanence.
Grasp.
Eye/hand coordination.
Shape and size discrimination.
Problem solving.
Emotional development.
Social interaction.
Concept of sharing.

- At around 12 months of age, your baby can blow a whistle. Encourage this play as it stimulates and strengthens the muscles of the mouth and face, as well as movements of the tongue. All these are important precursors in the development of speech and language. This play also instills cause and effect in the baby.

Masyog

As your baby is growing up, he will start to enjoy the massage and yoga stretches more and more. Masyog routines will give more flexibility to muscles and joints and will greatly help crawling, standing ,walking and balancing.

For more details please refer to the chapter on Masyog.

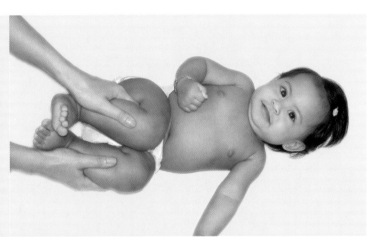

Balancing and Rocking

For more details please refer to the chapter on Balancing and Rocking.

Sign ✋ Language

Prerequisites for Sign Language remain the same as previous quarters, with the addition of the following.

Up — Point the index finger upward.

Down — Point the index finger downward.

Book — With both hands together open and close your palms.

No — The first two fingers of the hand are held together and opened and closed a few times against the extended thumb.

Stop	Car
☞ Stop - Hold out an open hand flat with the other hand coming down on it sideways.	☞ Car - Hold both fists at chest level and move in opposite directions as if turning a steering wheel.

❖ ⌘ ❖ ⌘ ❖ ⌘ ❖ ⌘ ❖

For more details please refer to the chapter on Sign Language.

Stimulation of the Right Brain
(Fourth Quarter)

Objectives of the Right Brain Stimulation

Image Visualization

High Speed mass memorization (Photographic Memory)

High Speed processing of information

Prerequisites of right brain stimulation are the same as the previous quarters.

Sequence of Flash Cards

Following is the chart for the **Flash Cards** that will be used in the tenth, eleventh and twelfth month. They have been grouped into different categories to be presented to the baby in an orderly routine.

Category	Number of Flash cards	Type
Animals	Twenty Four	Any 24 animals
Fruits and Vegetables	Twenty Four	Any 24 fruits and vegetables
Colors	Twelve	Red, Blue, Yellow, Green, Orange, Purple, Pink, Brown Grey, Black, Silver & Gold
Alphabets	Twenty Six	A to Z
Words	Twenty Four	Any 24 words
Common Objects	Twenty Four	Any 24 objects
Shapes	Twelve	Circle, triangle, square, rectangle, oval, diamond, trapezoid, cross, star Pentagon, Hexagon & Octagon
Numbers	Ten	1 to 10
Dots	Fifty	1-50 dot cards

In the tenth, eleventh & twelfth months, we will be showing a total of 206 Flash Cards which include the 150 cards from the previous quarters.

To make it even easier for the parent/caregiver or the program instructor, the categories have been divided into two groups.

Group 1 contains 110 Flash Cards, and Group 2 contains 96 Flash Cards.

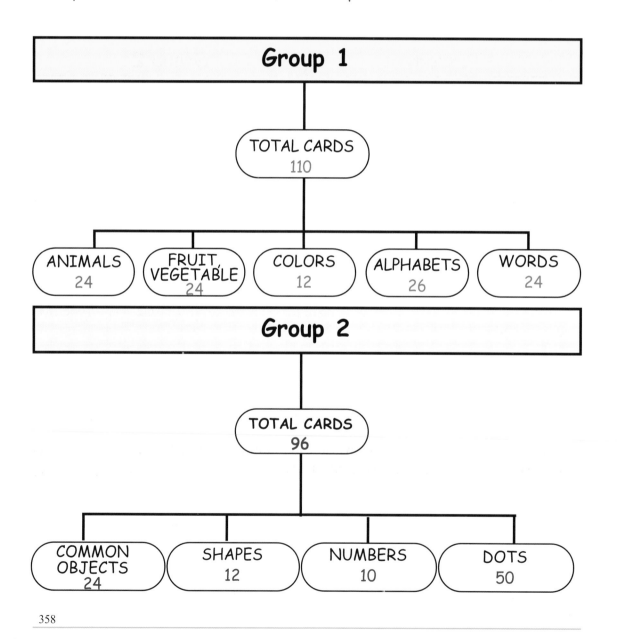

Schedule for the presentation of the
Flash Cards

Day	Group
Monday	Group 1
Tuesday	Group 2
Wednesday	Group 1
Thursday	Group 2
Friday	Group 1
Saturday	Group 2
Sunday	Group 1

⌗ As stressed earlier, the Flash Cards have to be shown rapidly at the rate of one card per second.

⌗ The cards have to be shown in two sessions through the course of the day.

⌗ There are no hard and fast rules pertaining to the specific order in which to show the Flash Cards. It is advisable to follow a pattern and keep changing the sequence.

⌗ In the case of the dot cards, it is advisable to follow a sequence for at least a few weeks in the beginning. Once you are confident that the baby is concentrating and responding well, you might want to try a random sequence.

⌗ Dot cards are very important for the development of counting and calculating abilities of the right brain.

⌗ You can show the baby all the cards in a single session, but it is recommended that you take a short break between different categories. This helps the baby retain interest and concentration.

¤ Looking at our table we know that on Monday we will be using flash cards from Group 1:

24 animals

24 fruits & vegetables

12 colors

26 alphabets

24 words

Total of 110 flash cards.

¤ Similarly, on Tuesday we will be showing flash cards from Group 2:

24 common objects

12 shapes

10 numbers

50 dots.

Total of 96 Flash Cards.

The Flash Card sequence should be repeated twice every day.

ଔ-ଈଔ-ଏଔ-ଈଔ

References

B. Worthington Roberts and S.R.Williams. - Nutrition in Pregnancy and Lactation. 5th edition. St.Louis: Mosby (1993)

Dennis. W. - Causes of retardation among institutional children. Journal of Genetic Psychology (1960).

Ainsworth, M.D.S. - Infancy in Uganda . Baltimore: John Hopkins Press (1967)

Crinic, L.S. - Effects of Nutrition and Environment on Brain Biochemistry and Behavior. Developmental Psychology. Vol.16 (1983).

.

Coursin, D.B. - Nutrition and Brain Development in Infants. Merril-Palmer Quaterly Vol 2 (1972).

Thomas Verny, with John Kelly. - The Secret Life of the Unborn Child. New York. Dell Publishing.

Kolata, G. - Studying Learning in the Womb. Science, Vol 225 (1984).

Bradley, R.M., Mistretta, C.M. - Fetal Sensory Receptors. Physiological Reviews, Vol. 55 (1975).

Salk L.. - The Role of the Heartbeat in the Relations between Mother and Infant. Scientific American. Vol 220 (1973)

Detterman, D.K. - The Effect of Heartbeat sound on Neonatal Crying. Infant behavior and development Vol 6 (1983)

Lamb, M.E., Campos, J.J. - Development in Infancy. New York: Random House. (1982).

Bruner, J. - Child's Talk: Learning to Use Language. New York .W.W.Norton and Company. (1983).

Lieberman, P. - The Biology and Evolution of Language.Cambridge. Harvard University Press. (1984).

Don Campbell. - The Mozart Effect for Children. London U.K. Hodder and Stoughton. (2002).

Acredolo, L. and S. Goodwyn. - Baby Signs.Chicago. Contemporary Books. (1996).

M.Jacobson. - Developmental Neurobiology.3rd edition.New York: Plenium (1991).

Dobbing, J. Sand, J. - The Quantitative Growth and Development of the Human Brain. Archives of Diseases of Children. Vol.48 (1974).

Makoto Shichida. - Children Can Change By The Right Brain Education. Shichida Child Education.Japan. (1998).

Makoto Shichida. - Babies Are Geniuses. Shichida Child Education.Japan. (1993).

ෆ෪ෆ෮ෆ෪ෆ